THE HUGE, HYSTERICAL, NEVER TERRIBLE BOOK OF Jokes FOR KiDS

3 BOOKS IN 1

WRITTEN BY
CAROLE P. ROMAN | CORINNE SCHMITT

callisto
publishing
an imprint of Sourcebooks

Copyright © 2024 by Callisto Publishing LLC
Cover and internal design © 2024 by Callisto Publishing LLC
Illustrations © Dylan Goldberger
Art Director: Eric Pratt, Erin Yeung, and Linda Snorina
Art Producer: Stacey Stambaugh
Editor: Erum Khan and Erin Nelson
Production Editor: Rachel Taenzler
Production Manager: Martin Worthington

Callisto Kids and the colophon are registered trademarks of Callisto Publishing LLC.

All rights reserved. No part of this book may be reproduced in any form or by any electronic or mechanical means including information storage and retrieval systems—except in the case of brief quotations embodied in critical articles or reviews—without permission in writing from its publisher, Sourcebooks LLC.

This book is a work of humor and intended for entertainment purposes only.

Published by Callisto Publishing LLC C/O Sourcebooks LLC
P.O. Box 4410, Naperville, Illinois 60567-4410
(630) 961-3900
callistopublishing.com

Originally published as *The Big Book of Silly Jokes for Kids* in 2019, *The Big Book of Silly Jokes for Kids 2* in 2020, and *The Big Book of Tricky Riddles for Kids* in 2020 in the United States of America by Callisto Kids, an imprint of Callisto Publishing LLC. This edition issued based on the paperback editions published in 2019 and 2020 in the United States of America by Callisto Kids, an imprint of Callisto Publishing LLC.

This product conforms to all applicable CPSC and CPSIA standards.

Source of Production: P.A. Hutchinson Company
Date of Production: August 2024
Run Number: 5041989

Printed and bound in the United States of America.
PAH 10 9 8 7 6 5 4 3 2 1

The Big Book of Silly Jokes for Kids

800+ Knock-Knocks, Tongue Twisters, Silly Stats, and More!

By Carole P. Roman

Illustrations by
Dylan Goldberger

To my dad.
He always knew
how to lighten
any situation
with a good joke.

LAUGHTER

is The Shortest Distance Between Two People.

—Victor Borge

Contents

Howdy, jokester!

Sometimes big laughs come in small packages. While *The Big Book of Silly Jokes for Kids* is something you can hold in one hand or pop into your backpack, it's also something I hope will give you laughs for years to come.

I wrote this book thinking of the fun you and your family might share after a long day. Many of these jokes have become staples in my own family, making everyone from grandkid to grandma giggle with glee. We are all so busy that the simple pleasure of exchanging a funny story, or having a rapid-fire pun contest is something special I wanted to celebrate in these pages.

So, whether you are looking to give your friends a knee-slapper with a knock-knock joke, stump a grown-up with a riddle, practice your comedian skills with a tricky tongue twister, or chuckle quietly to a run of jokes in your room, this book is meant for you . . . and all of your funny bones.

1

HA! Q&A

No matter where we live or what language we speak, one of the most important things we have in common is humor. When people laugh at a joke, many of our differences disappear.

Jokes can be a single question or even a story. What makes a joke so funny? Jokes surprise us with unexpected twists. They get us to look closely at words and figure out what they mean. When we suddenly get it, the surprise tickles our funny bone.

Many jokes have been told and retold so often that we don't know who actually thought of them. They belong to us all. Can you think of the last funny joke you heard? It's your joke to tell now!

You know how to laugh and make others laugh, so let's get to some joke cracking.

**What's a pirate's favorite
letter of the alphabet?**

ARRRRGH!

Who's the queen of the pencil case?
The ruler.

**What time do you
go to the dentist?**
Tooth-hurty.

**What did the nose
say to the finger?**
"Quit picking on me!"

Silly Stat: Just like fingerprints, tooth prints are unique to each person. They are as individual as you are!

**What did the left eye
say to the right eye?**
"Between us,
something smells."

**How do you make
a tissue dance?**
You put a little boogie in it.

**What time is it when
the clock strikes 13?**
Time to get a new clock.

**How do we know that
the ocean is friendly?**
It waves!

Why did the kid cross the playground?

To get to the other slide.

What is a tornado's favorite game to play?

Twister.

What falls in winter but never gets hurt?

Snow!

When does a joke become a "dad" joke?

When the punchline is a parent.

How do you stop an astronaut's baby from crying?

You rocket!

How are false teeth like stars?

They come out at night!

Why couldn't the astronaut book a hotel on the moon?

Because it was full.

Silly Stat: The distance from the moon to the earth is about roughly 238,900 miles. It takes about three days to travel from the earth to the moon.

How does the moon cut his hair?

Eclipse it.

What did the man say when he walked into a bar?

"Ouch!"

What has four wheels and flies?

A garbage truck.

How do you throw a party in space?

You planet.

What are the strongest days of the week?

Saturday and Sunday. Every other day is a weak day.

Why are robots never afraid?
They have nerves of steel.

Why are pirates, pirates?
Because they just arrrrgh!

**Why did the kid bring
a ladder to school?**
Because she wanted
to go to high school.

**What did one ocean
say to another ocean
when it asked the
other out on a date?**
"Shore."

**Why are shoemakers
such kind people?**
Because they have
good soles.

**Why did the kid
bury the battery?**
Because it was dead.

**Why couldn't the pirate
learn the alphabet?**
Because he was
always lost at "c."

Silly Stat: Pirates weren't just men. There were female pirates, too. Grace O'Malley, Mary Read, Anne Bonny, and Ching Shih were some famous women who looked for treasure at sea.

What do elves learn in school?

The elf-abet.

Where do pencils go on vacation?

Pencil-vania.

What building in New York has the most stories?

The public library.

What did the tween give his mom?

Ughs and kisses!

Why was the student's report card wet?

Because it was below "C" level.

What did one volcano say to the other?

"I lava you!"

Why didn't the dog want to play football?

It was a boxer!

What musical instrument is found in the bathroom?

A tuba toothpaste.

What did the big flower say to the little flower?

"Hi, bud!"

Kid: What are you doing under there?

Mom: Under where?
Kid: Ha! You said underwear!

Which flower will tell all your secrets?
Tulips.

What do you call a funny mountain?
Hill-arious.

What gets wetter the more it dries?
A towel.

What's brown, has no legs, but has a head and tail?
A penny.

Silly Stat: Pennies were one of the first coins minted in the United States. Do you know which American president's head is on the penny? (*Hint:* He was very tall!)

What did the book put on when it was cold?
A jacket.

Why did the man put his money in the freezer?
He wanted cold, hard cash.

How did the phone propose to its girlfriend?
It gave her a ring.

What did the painter say to her sweetheart?
"I love you with all my art."

What did one snowman say to another snowman?
"You're cool."

Why is there a gate around cemeteries?

Because people are dying to get in!

What stays in the corner yet can travel all over the world?

A stamp.

What do planets like to read?

Comet books.

What do you call an older snowman?

Water.

What do lawyers wear to court?

Lawsuits.

What has one head, one foot, and four legs?

A bed.

Why does Humpty Dumpty love autumn?
Because he always has a great fall.

**What word is always
spelled wrong in
the dictionary?**
Wrong.

**What did one snowman
say to the other snowman?**
"Wanna chill?"

**What do snowmen take
when the sun gets too hot?**
A chill pill.

**Why did the scarecrow
win an award?**
She was the best in her field.

**Where does a snowman
keep his money?**
In a snowbank.

**What kind of award did
the dentist receive?**
A little plaque.

**What kind of ball
doesn't bounce?**
A snowball.

**Why was the little
boy so cold?**
Because it was
Decembrrrrr!

What is the coldest country in the world?

Chile.

What has a bow but can't be tied?

A rainbow.

What is the best day to go to the beach?

Sunday.

What did the picture say to the wall?

"Do you mind if I hang around?"

What else did the picture say to the wall?

"Help! I've been framed."

What's the best season to jump on a trampoline?

Spring time.

Why did the girl go to bed with a pen?

To draw the curtains.

Why is dark spelled with a "k" and not a "c?"

Because you can't "c" in the dark.

How do you make fire with two sticks?

Make sure they are a match!

What's a balloon's least favorite type of music?

Pop.

Silly Stat: The trampoline was introduced to the public in Central Park, New York City, with a kangaroo jumping on it.

Why were they called the Dark Ages?

Because there were lots of knights.

Which rock group has four guys who can't sing or play instruments?

Mount Rushmore.

Want to hear a roof joke?

The first one's on the house.

How do hair stylists speed up their job?

They take shortcuts.

What did the goat ask for at the barbershop?

"A goatee trim for me!"

Silly Stat: Did you know the barbershop was an important part of the American civil rights movement? The barbershop was a place for community members to get together, share news, and spread the word.

Who can shave six times a day and still have a beard?

A barber.

What has only one eye, but still can't see?

A needle.

Why was the broom late?

It over-swept.

What starts and ends with "e" but has only one letter in it?

Envelope.

Where can you always find a tiger's head?

A few feet from its tail.

Where do sheep go on vacation?

To the Baaaaaahamas.

What can you catch but never throw?

A cold.

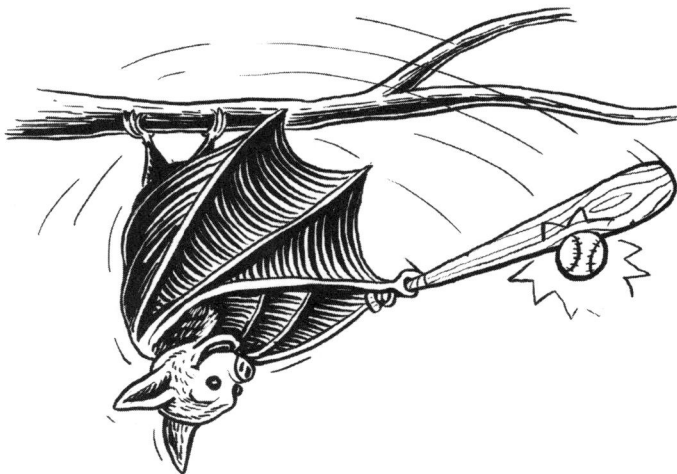

What animal is best at hitting a baseball?
A bat.

What did the girlfriend say to the billy goat?
"You have goat to be kidding me."

What did the baseball glove say to the ball?
"Catch you later."

I couldn't figure out why the baseball kept getting bigger ...
Then it hit me.

What runs around a baseball field but never moves?
The fence.

What did the football coach say to the broken vending machine?
"I want my quarterback!"

What do you call a secret group of llamas?
The I-llama-nati (*Illuminati*).

What did the llama say to the sad camel?

"Don't worry, you'll get over this hump."

What's more amazing than a talking llama?

A spelling bee!

How is a baseball team similar to a pancake?

They both need a good batter.

Why is a baseball stadium always cool?

It is full of fans.

When is a baseball player like a spider?

When he catches a fly!

Why do basketball players love doughnuts?

Because they can dunk 'em!

Why did the golfer wear two pairs of pants?

In case she got a hole-in-one.

What did the astronaut say when he crashed into the moon?

"I Apollo-gize."

What has 18 legs and catches flies?

A baseball team.

What kinds of stories do volleyball players tell?

Tall tales!

What is harder to catch the faster you run?

Your breath.

You know what's odd?

Every other number!

How can you tell if a plant is a math plant?
Because of its square roots.

What is a bird's favorite type of math?
Owl-gebra.

Why did the two fours not want any dinner?
Because they already eight!

Why is six afraid of seven?
Because seven ate nine.

What did the zero say to the eight?
"Nice belt."

Why was the math book unhappy?
Because it had too many problems!

What did the triangle say to the circle?
"You're pointless."

How do you make seven an even number?
Remove the "s."

Why did the obtuse angle go to the beach?
Because it was over 90 degrees.

Why was the math lesson so long?

Because the teacher kept going off on a tangent.

What did the mother angle say to her baby?

"Aww, what acute angle."

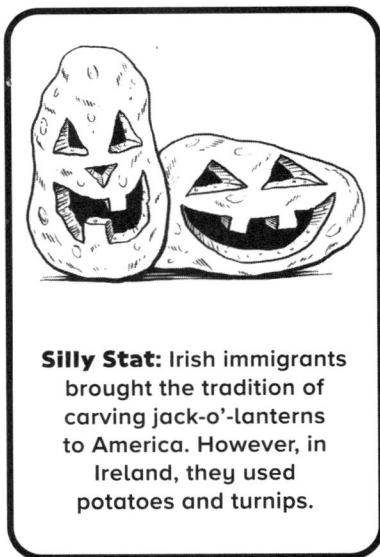

Silly Stat: Irish immigrants brought the tradition of carving jack-o'-lanterns to America. However, in Ireland, they used potatoes and turnips.

Why shouldn't you argue with a decimal?

Because decimals always have a point.

Why should you not talk to pi?

Because it will go on forever.

What do you get when you divide the circumference of a jack-o'-lantern by its diameter?

Pumpkin pi!

Want me to tell you a joke about pizza?

Sorry, it's too cheesy.

Why did the girl toss a stick of butter?

She wanted to see a butterfly.

What do you call cheese that isn't yours?

Nacho cheese.

What is a smartphone's favorite snack?

Computer chips!

What kind of tree fits in your hand?
A palm tree.

Silly Stat: Native American tribes were known to bend growing trees on purpose to mark trails. Many can be found today as hidden monuments.

What has ears but cannot hear?
A cornfield.

What's the worst vegetable to have on a ship?
A leek.

What is fast, loud, and crunchy?
A rocket chip!

Why did the student eat her homework?
Because the teacher said it was a piece of cake.

What did one plate say to the other plate?
"Dinner is on me."

How do pickles enjoy a day out?
They relish it.

What room can you never enter?
A mushroom.

**What did the cucumber
say to the pickle?**
"You mean a great
dill to me."

**What do you call two
banana peels?**
Slippers.

**Why didn't the orange
win the race?**
It ran out of juice.

**Why do bananas put
on suntan lotion?**
Because they don't
want to peel.

**Why did the cookie
go to the doctor?**
Because he felt crummy.

**Why did the banana
go to the doctor?**
Because it wasn't
peeling well.

Why did the tomato blush?

Because it saw the salad dressing.

Why did the lettuce win the race?

Because it was a head.

When do you stop at green and go at red?

When you're eating a watermelon.

Why didn't the robot finish his breakfast?

Because the orange juice told him to concentrate.

Why did Mozart sell his chickens?

They kept saying, "Bach, Bach, Bach."

What did the hamburger give her sweetheart?

An onion ring.

How do you fix a cracked jack-o'-lantern?

Give it a pumpkin patch.

What fruit do scarecrows love the most?

Strawberries.

How do ghosts wash their hair?

With sham-boo!

What is a ghost's favorite dessert?

I scream.

What kinds of pants do ghosts wear?

Boo jeans.

What room does a ghost not use?

A living room.

What do you call a snake in a bakery?

A pie-thon.

**What do you call a
ghost's true love?**
Their ghoul-friend.

**Where do baby ghosts
go during the day?**
To day-scare centers!

**What is a ghost's
nose full of?**
Boooooo-gers!

Why are ghosts bad liars?
Because you can see
right through them.

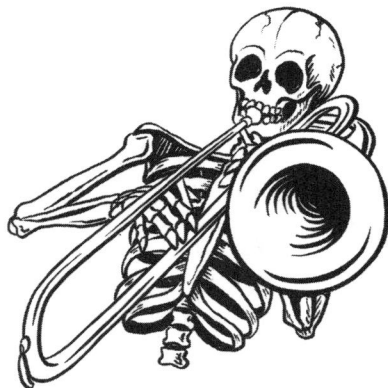

**What instrument does
a skeleton play?**
The trombone.

**Why didn't the
skeleton take his
friend to the prom?**
His heart wasn't in it.

**Why didn't the skeleton
cross the road?**
Because he didn't
have the guts.

**Why didn't the skeleton
go to the dance?**
He had no body
to dance with.

**What do you call a witch
who goes to the beach?**
A sand-witch.

**What is a witch's favorite
subject in school?**
Spelling.

**What do you call two
witches who live together?**
Broom-mates.

What do birds say on Halloween?
"Trick or tweet!"

**What do vampires
give you in winter?**
Frostbite!

**What monster is
the best artist?**
Dracula, because he
likes to draw blood.

**How can you tell a
vampire has a cold?**
He starts coffin.

**What monster plays
tricks on Halloween?**
Prank-enstein!

**What is a vampire's
favorite fruit?**
A blood orange.

**What kind of music
do mummies love?**
Wrap music.

**How does a vampire
start a letter?**
Tomb it may concern . . .

**What did the farmer
give his family for
Valentine's Day?**
Hogs and kisses.

What did the stamp say to the envelope on Valentine's Day?

"I'm stuck on you."

What do you write in a slug's Valentine's Day card?

Be my valen-slime.

Why do skunks love Valentine's Day?

They are very scent-imental creatures.

What happened when the Easter bunny didn't behave in school?

He was egg-spelled.

What did one lightbulb say to the other lightbulb?

"I wuv you watts and watts!"

Why do mummies like birthdays so much?

Because of all the wrapping!

Which is the best hand to light the Hanukkah menorah?

Neither. It's best to use a candle.

What do you call a greedy elf?

Elfish.

What do you say to an octopus on Valentine's Day?

"I want to hold your hand, hand, hand, hand, hand, hand, hand, hand!"

Why do bees hum?

Because they don't know the words.

What is a cow's favorite holiday?
Moo Year's Day.

**What comes at the end
of Christmas Day?**
The letter "y."

**What did the
gingerbread man put
under his blankets?**
A cookie sheet.

**What do you call Santa
when he stops moving?**
Santa Pause.

**What should you never
eat on July 4th?**
Firecrackers.

What do you call an alligator wearing a vest?
An investigator.

What do you call a sleeping dinosaur?
A dino-snore.

Why don't dinosaurs eat clowns?
Because they taste funny.

What do owls say to declare their love?
"Owl be yours."

Why does a seagull fly over the sea?
Because if it flew over the bay, it would be a bay-gull.

Why don't koalas count as bears?
They don't have the right koala-fications.

Why do bees have sticky hair?
Because they use a honeycomb.

What kind of haircuts do bees get?
Buzzzzz cuts.

What did the bee say to the flower?
"Hi, honey."

**What did one bee
say to the other?**

"I love bee-ing with you."

**What do you call
a clever bee?**

A spelling bee.

**What's worse than finding
a worm in your apple?**

Finding half a worm.

**Why did the ants
dance on the jam jar?**

Because the lid said,
"Twist to open."

**What do you get when
you cross a centipede
with a parrot?**

A walkie-talkie.

**How do you know
a squirrel has had
too much candy?**

It's acting like a nut.

**What do you call a
bear that jumps but
never lands?**

Peter Panda.

**What do you get when
you cross an elephant
and a potato?**

Mashed potatoes.

**What do you call
two birds in love?**

Tweet-hearts.

**What do you get
when you cross an
elephant with a fish?**

Swimming trunks.

**What kind of pillar can't
hold up a building?**

A caterpillar.

What time is it when an elephant sits on your fence?

Time to get a new fence.

Silly Stat: Did you know that elephants can't jump? But they're not the only ones. Rhinoceroses, hippopotamuses, and sloths can't jump either.

Where would you find an elephant?

The same place that you lost her.

Where do elephants pack their clothes?

In their trunks.

How do you stop an elephant from charging?

Take away his credit card.

What did the wolf say when it stubbed its toe?
"Howwwwwl!"

How do you know that carrots are good for your eyesight?
Have you ever seen a rabbit with glasses?

What kind of shoes do frogs wear?
Open toad shoes.

Why did the chewing gum cross the road?
It was stuck to the chicken's foot.

Why do farmers put bells on cows?
Their horns don't make noise.

What do dogs do when watching Netflix?

They press paws.

What did the banana say to the dog?

Nothing. Bananas can't talk.

Why aren't dogs good dancers?

They have two left feet.

What kind of key can never unlock a door?

A monkey.

What goes *tick-tock* and *woof-woof*?

A watchdog.

What do you call a monkey that loves potato chips?

A chip-monk.

What happened when the skunk was on trial?

The judge declared, "Odor in the court, odor in the court!"

What do you get when you cross a dog with a telephone?

A golden receiver.

Where do dogs park?

In a barking lot.

What did the Dalmatian say after lunch?

"That hit the spot."

What do you call a sleeping bull?

A bulldozer.

Why can't you play hockey with pigs?

They always hog the puck.

Why do porcupines always win the game?

They have the most points.

What do you call a bear with no teeth?

A gummy bear.

Why did the teddy bear say "no" to dessert?

Because he was stuffed.

What do you call a pig that knows karate?

Pork chop.

What do you call a duck that gets all "A's"?

A wise-quacker.

How do you make a jellyfish laugh?

With ten-tickles!

Silly Stat: A common mistake is to think an octopus has tentacles. Scientifically speaking, an octopus has eight arms and zero tentacles!

Why wouldn't the crab share his treasure?

Because he was a little shellfish.

Why did they quit giving tests at the zoo?

Because it was full of cheetahs.

Why couldn't the pony sing a lullaby?

She was a little hoarse.

What do you call a fish without an eye?

A fsssssh.

How many South Americans does it take to change a lightbulb?

A Brazilian.

Why was there thunder and lightning in the lab?

They were brainstorming.

Why did the tree go to the dentist?

To get a root canal.

What goes up and down but doesn't move?

Stairs.

What do you call a dog magician?

A Labra-ca-dabra-dor.

What's black and white and red all over?

An embarrassed zebra.

Why did the police officer go to the baseball game?

She heard someone had stolen a base.

What kind of car does Mickey Mouse's girlfriend drive?

A Minnie van.

What do you call a happy cowboy?

A jolly rancher.

Why couldn't the pirate play cards?

Because he was sitting on the deck.

What letters are not in the alphabet?

The ones in the mail.

Why do fish live in salt water?

Because pepper makes them sneeze.

How does a train eat?

It goes chew-chew.

Where do young cows eat lunch?

In the calf-eteria.

What type of markets do dogs avoid?

Flea markets.

What's a cat's favorite color?

Purrr-ple.

Silly Stat: Laughter is good for you! It decreases the chemicals in our bodies that make us sick and increases the ones that make us feel better.

How do you make gold soup?

Put 24 carrots in it.

What time do ducks wake up?

At the quack of dawn.

What kind of bird works at a construction site?

A crane.

2

KNOCK, KNOCK

Can you think back to the first joke you ever told? There is a good chance it was a knock-knock joke. You might even feel like you were born knowing how to knock, knock.

Knock-knock jokes first became popular in America in the 1920s, but they are told all over the world. In French, the joke starts with "toc, toc." In Afrikaans and Dutch, it's "klop, klop." In Korean and Japanese, it's "kon, kon." And in Spanish, knock-knock jokes often rhyme!

Knock-knock jokes are fun because they always follow the same format. Most of them are short and easy to remember. In fact, once you start doing them, it's hard to stop!

KNOCK, KNOCK.

WHO'S THERE?

GORILLA.

GORILLA WHO?
GORILLA ME A HOTDOG, WILL YOU?

Knock, knock.
Who's there?
You.
You who?
Yoo-hoo, it's your turn!

Knock, knock.
Who's there?
Aardvark.
Aardvark who?
**Aardvark a hundred miles
for you.**

Knock, knock.
Who's there?
Honey bee.
Honey bee who?
Honey bee good!

> **Silly Stat:** Did you know
> that insects are considered
> a good source of nutrition
> for some animals, even
> humans? Most of them are
> rich in protein, healthy fats,
> iron, and calcium, and low
> in carbohydrates. Many
> countries include insects
> as an essential part of their
> daily diet. What bugs would
> you be willing to try?

Knock, knock.
Who's there?
Alli.
Alli who?
Alligator.

Knock, knock.
Who's there?
A herd.
A herd who?
**A herd you were home,
so I came over.**

Knock, knock.
Who's there?
Lion.
Lion who?
Lion bed, sleepyhead.

Knock, knock.
Who's there?
Cow-go.
Cow-go who?
Cow-go, "Moo, moo."

Knock, knock.
Who's there?
Ruff.
Ruff who?
Ruff, ruff, it's your dog.

Knock, knock.
Who's there?
Thumpin'.
Thumpin' who?
**There's thumpin' furry
crawling up your back.**

Knock, knock.
Who's there?
Doughnut.
Doughnut who?
**Doughnut leave before
you walk the dog.**

Knock, knock.
Who's there?
Iguana.
Iguana who?
Iguana hold your hand.

Knock, knock.
Who's there?
Owl.
Owl who?
**Owl-gebra class
is my favorite!**

Knock, knock.
Who's there?
Chick.
Chick who?
**Chick your shoelaces,
they're untied.**

Knock, knock.
Who's there?
Alpaca.
Alpaca who?
**Alpaca suitcase,
you pack a lunch!**

Knock, knock.
Who's there?
Moose.
Moose who?
**Moose you tell these
knock-knock jokes?**

Knock, knock.
Who's there?
Giraffe.
Giraffe who?
Giraffe anything to eat?
I'm hungry.

Knock, knock.
Who's there?
Owls.
Owls who?
Why yes, they do.

Knock, knock.
Who's there?
Moo.
Moo who?
Aww, don't cry, baby calf.

Knock, knock.
Who's there?
Toucan.
Toucan who?
Toucan play that game.

Knock, knock.
Who's there?
Viper.
Viper who?
Viper nose, it's running.

Knock, knock.
Who's there?
Beats.
Beats who?
Beats me.

Knock, knock.
Who's there?
Ice cream.
Ice cream who?
Ice cream with happiness!

Knock, knock.
Who's there?
Cash.
Cash who?
No thanks, I want almonds.

Knock, knock.
Who's there?
Lettuce.
Lettuce who?
Lettuce in, it's cold out here!

Knock, knock.
Who's there?
Eggs.
Eggs who?
Egg-cited to see you.

Knock, knock.
Who's there?
Mustard.
Mustard who?
Mustard you knocking.

Knock, knock.
Who's there?
Broccoli.
Broccoli who?
Broccoli doesn't have a last name, silly!

Knock, knock.
Who's there?
Pecan.
Pecan who?
Pecan somebody your own size.

Knock, knock.
Who's there?
Math.
Math who?
Can you pass the math potatoes?

Knock, knock.
Who's there?
Yam.
Yam who?
I yam what I am.

Knock, knock.
Who's there?
Doughnut.
Doughnut who?
**Doughnut ask where
the treasure is!**
It's a secret.

Knock, knock.
Who's there?
Soup.
Soup who?
Souperwoman!

Knock, knock.
Who's there?
Bean.
Bean who?
Bean there, done that.

Knock, knock.
Who's there?
Seed.
Seed who?
Seed you tomorrow.

Knock, knock.
Who's there?
Olive.
Olive who?
Olive you a lot.

Knock, knock.
Who's there?
Jello.
Jello who?
Jello, is anybody home?

Knock, knock.
Who's there?
Poodle.
Poodle who?
**Poodle little ketchup
on my burger.**

Knock, knock.
Who's there?
Barbie.
Barbie who?
Barbie Q. Chicken.

Knock, knock.
Who's there?
Pete.
Pete who?
Pete-za delivery.

Knock, knock.
Who's there?
Pasta.
Pasta who?
Pasta salt, please.

Silly Stat: In 2005, scientists found a four-thousand-year-old bowl of pasta in China. The long, thin yellow noodles were buried 10 feet below ground and made from two different kinds of millet, a tasty grain!

Knock, knock.
Who's there?
Bunny.
Bunny who?
Some bunny been eating my carrots.

Knock, knock.
Who's there?
Plato.
Plato who?
Plato fish and chips.

Knock, knock.
Who's there?
Peas.
Peas who?
Peas pass the butter.

Knock, knock.
Who's there?
Handsome.
Handsome who?
Handsome mustard to me, please.

Knock, knock.
Who's there?
Noah.
Noah who?
Noah good restaurant around here?

Knock, knock.
Who's there?
Turnip.
Turnip who?
Turnip the music!

Knock, knock.
Who's there?
Nacho.
Nacho who?
**That's nacho sandwich.
It's mine!**

Silly Stat: Did you know
that November 6th is
National Nacho Day? Mark
your calendar and dig in to
your favorite cheesy snack.

Knock, knock.
Who's there?
Theresa.
Theresa who?
Theresa fly in my soup.

Knock, knock.
Who's there?
Butter.
Butter who?
Butter let me in soon.

Knock, knock.
Who's there?
Cheese.
Cheese who?
Cheese such a sweet girl.

Knock, knock.
Who's there?
Cereal.
Cereal who?
**Cereal pleasure
to meet you.**

Knock, knock.
Who's there?
Ketchup.
Ketchup who?
**Ketchup with me
and I'll tell you!**

Knock, knock.
Who's there?
Figs.
Figs who?
**Figs the doorbell, please.
It's broken.**

Knock, knock.
Who's there?
Four eggs.
Four eggs who?
Four eggs-ample, it's me.

Knock, knock.
Who's there?
Dee.
Dee who?
**Dee-licious cookies
for sale.**

Knock, knock.
Who's there?
Orange.
Orange who?
**Orange you gonna
let me in?**

> **Silly Stat:** A bunch of
> bananas are called a hand.

Knock, knock.
Who's there?
Banana.
Banana who?
Knock, knock.
Who's there?
Banana.
Banana who?
Knock, knock.
Who's there?
Orange.
Orange who?
**Orange you glad
I didn't say banana?**

Knock, knock.
Who's there?
Berry.
Berry who?
Berry nice to meet you.

Knock, knock.
Who's there?
Abby.
Abby who?
Abby birthday to you!

Knock, knock.
Who's there?
Jamal.
Jamal who?
Jamal shook up.

Knock, knock.
Who's there?
Ada.
Ada who?
Ada sandwich for lunch.

Knock, knock.
Who's there?
Abby.
Abby who?
A, B, C, D, E, F, G.

Knock, knock.
Who's there?
Alfie.
Alfie who?
Alfie good about the test.

Knock, knock.
Who's there?
Zoom.
Zoom who?
Zoom do you think it is?

Knock, knock.
Who's there?
Alma.
Alma who?
Alma not going to say.

Knock, knock.
Who's there?
Annie.
Annie who?
**Annie body going
to the park?**

Knock, knock.
Who's there?
Spell.
Spell who?
Okay, okay: W-H-O.

Knock, knock.
Who's there?
Abel.
Abel who?
**Abel to leap tall buildings
in a single bound!**

Knock, knock.
Who's there?
Kanga.
Kanga who?
Actually, it's kangaroo.

Knock, knock.
Who's there?
Albert.
Albert who?
**Albert you can't guess
who I am.**

Knock, knock.
Who's there?
Alex.
Alex who?
**Alex the questions
around here.**

Knock, knock.
Who's there?
Alice.
Alice who?
Alice fair in love and war.

Knock, knock.
Who's there?
Dwayne.
Dwayne who?
**Dwayne the bathtub,
it's overflowing.**

Knock, knock.
Who's there?
Andrew.
Andrew who?
**Andrew a nice picture
for you.**

Knock, knock!
Who's there?
Candy.
Candy who?
**Candy cow really jump
over the moon?**

Knock, knock.
Who's there?
Annie.
Annie who?
Annie body home?

Knock, knock.
Who's there?
Annie.
Annie who?
**Annie more of these
knock-knock jokes?**

Knock, knock.
Who's there?
Annetta.
Annetta who?
**Annetta
knock-knock joke.**

Knock, knock.
Who's there?
Muffin.
Muffin who?
**Muffin the matter with
me, how about you?**

Knock, knock.
Who's there?
Barry.
Barry who?
Barry nice to see you.

Knock, knock.
Who's there?
Ben.
Ben who?
Ben there, done that.

Knock, knock.
Who's there?
Carmen.
Carmen who?
Carmen get it.

Knock, knock.
Who's there?
Colin.
Colin who?
**Colin all kids
to get some pasta!**

Knock, knock.
Who's there?
Constance.
Constance who?
**Constance waiting out
here anymore.**

Knock, knock.
Who's there?
Adore.
Adore who?
**Adore is between us.
Open up!**

Knock, knock.
Who's there?
Emma.
Emma who?
**Emma getting hungry.
When's dinner?**

Knock, knock.
Who's there?
Dawn.
Dawn who?
**Dawn forget your
backpack.**

Knock, knock.
Who's there?
Fanny.
Fanny who?
**Fanny body calls,
please tell them I'm out.**

Knock, knock.
Who's there?
Doris.
Doris who?
**Doris a bit squeaky,
do you have some oil?**

Knock, knock.
Who's there?
Fred.
Fred who?
**Who is a Fred of
the big bad wolf?**

Knock, knock.
Who's there?
Freddy.
Freddy who?
**Freddy or not,
here I come!**

Knock, knock.
Who's there?
Gus.
Gus who?
**That's what *you're*
supposed to do!**

Knock, knock.
Who's there?
Gwen.
Gwen who?
Gwen will I see you again?

Knock, knock.
Who's there?
Hal.
Hal who?
Hal-o, anybody home?

Knock, knock.
Who's there?
Frank.
Frank who?
**Frank you for answering
the door.**

Knock, knock.
Who's there?
Harry.
Harry who?
**Harry up, I want to go
to the beach!**

Knock, knock.
Who's there?
Howard.
Howard who?
Howard I know?

Knock, knock.
Who's there?
Hugh.
Hugh who?
**Hugh-who!
Don't you see me?**

Knock, knock.
Who's there?
Ida.
Ida who?
Ida like to dance to music!

Knock, knock.
Who's there?
Hugo.
Hugo who?
Hugo first, I'll go second.

Knock, knock.
Who's there?
Isabel.
Isabel who?
**Isabel necessary
for this door?**

Knock, knock.
Who's there?
Iris.
Iris who?
Iris you'd sing me a song.

Knock, knock.
Who's there?
Izzy.
Izzy who?
Izzy home?

Knock, knock.
Who's there?
Ivan.
Ivan who?
**Ivan working
on an invention.**

Knock, knock.
Who's there?
Kim.
Kim who?
Kim too late to the party.

Knock, knock.
Who's there?
Kanye.
Kanye who?
**Kanye make sure
to bring the pizza?**

Knock, knock.
Who's there?
Kent.
Kent who?
**Kent you tell who
I am by my voice?**

Knock, knock.
Who's there?
Jess.
Jess who?
Jess me, myself, and I.

Knock, knock.
Who's there?
Ken.
Ken who?
**Ken you come out
and play with me?**

Knock, knock.
Who's there?
Juno.
Juno who?
**Juno where Europe
is on the map?**

Knock, knock.
Who's there?
Justin.
Justin who?
**Justin the neighborhood
and I thought I'd visit.**

Knock, knock.
Who's there?
Lena.
Lena who?
**Lena little closer and
I'll tell you a secret.**

Knock, knock.
Who's there?
Luke.
Luke who?
**Luke out the window
and you'll see.**

Knock, knock.
Who's there?
Mandy.
Mandy who?
**Mandy lifeboats,
de ship is sinking!**

Knock, knock.
Who's there?
Thermos.
Thermos who?
**Thermos be a better
knock-knock joke
than this!**

Knock, knock.
Who's there?
Marge and Tina.
Marge and Tina who?
**Don't cry for me
Marge and Tina.**

Silly Stat: "Don't Cry for Me, Argentina" is a show-stopping song about Eva Perón's rise to power in the movie musical *Evita*. Do you know who sings it? Hint: She also sings the song "Like a Prayer."

Knock, knock.
Who's there?
Mikey.
Mikey who?
**Mikey won't fit
in the lock.**

Knock, knock.
Who's there?
Manny.
Manny who?
**Manny people want
to come over.**

Knock, knock.
Who's there?
May.
May who?
May I come in?

Knock, knock.
Who's there?
Nana.
Nana who?
Nana your business.

Knock, knock.
Who's there?
Paul.
Paul who?
**Paul up a chair
and I'll tell you.**

Knock, knock.
Who's there?
Perry.
Perry who?
**Perry well,
and how are you?**

Knock, knock.
Who's there?
Phyllis.
Phyllis who?
**Phyllis in on your
soccer game.**

Knock, knock.
Who's there?
Oliver.
Oliver who?
**Oliver troubles will be
over soon.**

Knock, knock.
Who's there?
Oswald.
Oswald who?
**Oswald my bubble gum.
Ick!**

Knock, knock.
Who's there?
Otto.
Otto who?
**Otto know what's
taking you so long.**

Knock, knock.
Who's there?
Rhoda.
Rhoda who?
**Row, row, Rhoda boat,
gently down the stream . . .**

Knock, knock.
Who's there?
Amos.
Amos who?
Amos-quito.

Knock, knock.
Who's there?
Sadie.
Sadie who?
**Sadie magic word
and I'll go away.**

Knock, knock.
Who's there?
Sara.
Sara who?
**Sara 'nother way
into this place?**

Knock, knock.
Who's there?
Scott.
Scott who?
**Scott nothing to do
with you.**

Knock, knock.
Who's there?
Seymour.
Seymour who?
**Seymour outside if you
open the curtain.**

Knock, knock.
Who's there?
Shelby.
Shelby who?
**Shelby comin' 'round the
mountain when she comes.**

Knock, knock.
Who's there?
Shirley.
Shirley who?
**Shirley you can tell
from my voice?**

Knock, knock.
Who's there?
Stu.
Stu who?
Stu late, it's time for bed!

Knock, knock.
Who's there?
Troy.
Troy who?
Troy the doorknob.

Knock, knock.
Who's there?
Tyrone.
Tyrone who?
Tyrone shoelaces!

Knock, knock.
Who's there?
Ringo.
Ringo who?
Ringo 'round the rosie.

Knock, knock.
Who's there?
Roland.
Roland who?
**A Roland stone
gathers no moss.**

Knock, knock.
Who's there?
Theodora.
Theodora who?
**Theodora is stuck and
the cat can't get out.**

> **Silly Stat:** In 1936, a
> newspaper published one of
> the first knock-knock jokes in
> print. It was an ad for a new
> roof. It went like this:
>
> Knock, knock.
> Who's there?
> **Rufus.**
> Rufus who?
> **Rufus the most important
> part of your house.**

Knock, knock.
Who's there?
Wayne.
Wayne who?
**Wayne drops are
falling on my head.**

Knock, knock.
Who's there?
Wendy.
Wendy who?
**Wendy wind blows,
the cradle will rock.**

Knock, knock.
Who's there?
Tamara.
Tamara who?
**Tamara is Monday,
today is Sunday.**

Knock, knock.
Who's there?
Will.
Will who?
**Will you go to the
party with me?**

Knock, knock.
Who's there?
Thea.
Thea who?
Thea tomorrow.

Knock, knock.
Who's there?
Yvonne.
Yvonne who?
Yvonne to be brave!

Knock, knock.
Who's there?
Zach.
Zach who?
Zach's all folks!

Knock, knock.
Who's there?
Mustache.
Mustache who?
I mustache you a question.

Knock, knock.
Who's there?
Amarillo.
Amarillo who?
Amarillo nice gal.

Knock, knock.
Who's there?
Alaska.
Alaska who?
Alaska the questions around here.

Knock, knock.
Who's there?
Candice.
Candice who?
Candice door open?

Knock, knock.
Who's there?
Havana.
Havana who?
Havana wonderful time and wish you were here.

Knock, knock.
Who's there?
Venice.
Venice who?
Venice your mom coming home?

Knock, knock.
Who's there?
Iowa.
Iowa who?
Iowa you a lot of candy!

Silly Stat: In the early part of the twentieth century knock-knock clubs formed in America in the states of Illinois, Iowa, and Kansas.

Knock, knock.
Who's there?
Juneau.
Juneau who?
Juneau what time it is?

Knock, knock.
Who's there?
Oslo.
Oslo who?
**Oslo down so
you can catch up.**

Knock, knock.
Who's there?
Jamaica.
Jamaica who?
Jamaica me a sandwich?

Knock, knock.
Who's there?
Rome.
Rome who?
Rome is where the heart is.

Knock, knock.
Who's there?
Norway.
Norway who?
**There's Norway I'm going
to leave without lunch.**

Knock, knock.
Who's there?
Paris.
*(Try to pronounce this in
French, "Pair-ee!")*
Paris who?
Paris nice to meet you.

Knock, knock.
Who's there?
Al.
Al who?
Al see you in Detroit!

Knock, knock.
Who's there?
Tibet.
Tibet who?
**Early Tibet and
early to rise.**

Knock, knock.
Who's there?
Pakistan.
Pakistan who?
**Pakistan-wich,
you might get hungry.**

Knock, knock.
Who's there?
Tennis.
Tennis who?
Tennis-see.

Knock, knock.
Who's there?
Yukon.
Yukon who?
Yukon say that again.

Knock, knock.
Who's there?
Tunis.
Tunis who?
**Tunis company,
three's a crowd.**

Knock, knock.
Who's there?
York.
York who?
York on the way home?

Knock, knock.
Who's there?
Mayan.
Mayan who?
**Mayan the force
be with you.**

Silly Stat: Yoda has three toes in *The Phantom Menace*. He's got four in *The Empire Strikes Back*, *Return of the Jedi*, and *Revenge of the Sith*.

Knock, knock.
Who's there?
Beth.
Beth who?
**Beth wishes for a
happy New Year.**

Knock, knock.
Who's there?
Freeze.
Freeze who?
Freeze a jolly good fellow.

Knock, knock.
Who's there?
Eye.
Eye who?
**Eye want to wish you
a happy New Year.**

Knock, knock.
Who's there?
Will.
Will who?
Will you be my Valentine?

Knock, knock.
Who's there?
Irish.
Irish who?
**Irish you a happy
St. Patrick's Day.**

Knock, knock.
Who's there?
Noah.
Noah who?
Noah body! April Fools!

Knock, knock.
Who's there?
Seder.
Seder who?
**Make sure you seder right
story at Passover dinner.**

Knock, knock.
Who's there?
Ana.
Ana who?
Ana-ther Easter bunny.

Knock, knock.
Who's there?
Kenya.
Kenya who?
**Kenya ask Mom for
another potato pancake?**

Silly Stat: Hanukkah,
the Jewish Festival of Lights,
is celebrated on a different
day every year.

Knock, knock.
Who's there?
Berlin.
Berlin who?
**Berlin (*boilin'*) the water
for the Easter eggs.**

Knock, knock.
Who's there?
Carrie.
Carrie who?
**Carrie my Halloween
candy, please.**

Knock, knock.
Who's there?
Bea.
Bea who?
Bea nice to your brother.

Knock, knock.
Who's there?
Bacon.
Bacon who?
**He's bacon brownies
for the bake sale.**

Knock, knock.
Who's there?
Ben.
Ben who?
**Ben waiting all year
for school to end.**

Knock, knock.
Who's there?
Sasha.
Sasha who?
**Sasha fancy
fireworks display.**

Knock, knock.
Who's there?
Boo hoo.
Boo hoo who?
**Oh, don't cry, it's just
a Halloween costume.**

Knock, knock.
Who's there?
Canoe.
Canoe who?
**Canoe watch the Fourth
of July fireworks?**

Knock, knock.
Who's there?
Phillip.
Phillip who?
**Please Phillip my bag
with candy!**

Knock, knock.
Who's there?
Tree.
Tree who?
Tree wise men.

Knock, knock.
Who's there?
Witch.
Witch who?
**Witch way to the
haunted house?**

Knock, knock.
Who's there?
Wanda.
Wanda who?
**Wanda go for a spin
on my broomstick?**

Knock, knock.
Who's there?
Witch.
Witch who?
**Witch one of you has
the best candy?**

Knock, knock.
Who's there?
Esther.
Esther who?
**Esther any more
mashed potatoes?**

Knock, knock.
Who's there?
Arthur.
Arthur who?
**Arthur any more
Thanksgiving leftovers?**

Knock, knock.
Who's there?
Dewey.
Dewey who?
**Dewey have to wait
long to eat?**

Knock, knock.
Who's there?
Eyewash.
Eyewash who?
**Eyewash you a
happy Ramadan.**

Silly Stat: Ramadan is a month-long time to fast and pray in the Islamic tradition. You can also say, "Ramadan Mubarak," which means "Happy Ramadan" or "Congratulations, it's Ramadan" in Arabic.

Knock, knock.
Who's there?
Annie.
Annie who?
**Annie body want
some turkey?**

Knock, knock.
Who's there?
Anita lift.
Anita lift who?
Anita lift, Rudolph.

Knock, knock.
Who's there?
Honda.
Honda who?
**Honda first day
of Christmas,
my true love sent to me . . .**

Knock, knock.
Who's there?
Alaska.
Alaska who?
**Alaska Santa for a
new bike.**

Knock, knock.
Who's there?
Europe.
Europe who?
**Europe-ning the door
too slowly!**

Knock, knock.
Who's there?
Mary.
Mary who?
Mary Christmas.

Knock, knock.
Who's there?
Gladys.
Gladys who?
Gladys Kwanzaa.

Silly Stat: Kwanzaa is a relatively new holiday that began in the United States in 1966 to honor the African-American community after the 1965 Watts riots in Los Angeles. This holiday is centered around the core principles of unity, self-determination, collective work and responsibility, cooperative economics, purpose, creativity, and faith.

Knock, knock.
Who's there?
Holly.
Holly who?
**The Holly-days
are here again!**

Knock, knock.
Who's there?
Harvey.
Harvey who?
**Harvey gonna play
some ball?**

Knock, knock.
Who's there?
Les.
Les who?
Les go play some golf.

Knock, knock.
Who's there?
Dozen.
Dozen who?
**Dozen-yone want to
play basketball?**

Knock, knock.
Who's there?
Meow.
Meow who?
**Take meow to the
ballgame.**

Knock, knock.
Who's there?
Canoe.
Canoe who?
**Canoe play some
video games?**

Knock, knock.
Who's there?
Wanda.
Wanda who?
Wanda play outside?

Knock, knock.
Who's there?
Gargoyle.
Gargoyle who?
**Gargoyle with saltwater
and your throat will
feel better.**

Knock, knock.
Who's there?
Tennis.
Tennis who?
**Tennis my favorite
number.**

Knock, knock.
Who's there?
Uriah.
Uriah who?
Keep Uriah the ball.

Knock, knock.
Who's there?
Wooden shoe.
Wooden shoe who?
**Wooden shoe like
to hear another
knock-knock joke?**

Knock, knock.
Who's there?
Broken pencil.
Broken pencil who?
Never mind, it's pointless.

Knock, knock.
Who's there?
Needle.
Needle who?
**Needle little help
answering the door?**

Knock, knock.
Who's there?
Sherlock.
Sherlock who?
Sherlock your bike.

Knock, knock.
Who's there?
A little old lady.
A little old lady who?
**I didn't know
you could yodel!**

Knock, knock.
Who's there?
Water.
Water who?
**Water you doing
right now?**

Knock, knock.
Who's there?
Lease.
Lease who?
**Lease you could do
is open the door!**

Knock, knock.
Who's there?
Rocket.
Rocket who?
**Rocket-bye baby,
on the treetop . . .**

Knock, knock.
Who's there?
Comb.
Comb who?
Comb on in and sit a bit.

Knock, knock.
Who's there?
Ifor.
Ifor who?
Ifor got!

Knock, knock.
Who's there?
Ima.
Ima who?
Ima make you a snack!

Knock, knock.
Who's there?
Radio.
Radio who?
Radio not, here I come!

Knock, knock.
Who's there?
Cargo.
Cargo who?
Cargo *vroom, vroom*.

Knock, knock.
Who's there?
Howl.
Howl who?
I'm fine, and howl you?

Knock, knock.
Who's there?
Jacken.
Jacken who?
**Jacken Jill went
up the hill.**

Knock, knock.
Who's there?
Tarzan.
Tarzan who?
**Tarzan stripes on the
American flag.**

Knock, knock.
Who's there?
Alien.
Alien who?
**How many aliens
do you know?**

Knock, knock.
Who's there?
Hada.
Hada who?
Hada great time.

Knock, knock.
Who's there?
Bed.
Bed who?
**Bed you can't guess
who this is.**

Knock, knock.
Who's there?
Scold.
Scold who?
**Scold outside.
Put on your jacket!**

Knock, knock.
Who's there?
Althea.
Althea who?
Althea later, alligator.

Knock, knock.
Who's there?
Sir.
Sir who?
**Sir-prise! I have
more jokes for you.**

3

Tongue Twisters

Tongue twisters serve a practical purpose when practicing pronunciation. (Do you see what I did there?)

They strengthen and stretch the muscles in your mouth and this makes it easier to say some of the toughest sounds. That's why everyone from actors to teachers uses them.

They're also silly. It's fun to challenge yourself, your family, and your friends to see how fast and how many times you can say a tongue twister. Hey, you could even host a **Tongue Twist-Off Tournament!**

SANTA'S

SHORT

SUIT

SHRUNK

As you practice, here's a trick to be the fastest twister master on your block.

1. Pick a tongue twister.
2. Write it down on a piece of paper.
3. Read it five times to yourself.
4. Whisper it at a normal speed.
5. Now read it out loud, very slowly, five times.
6. Do this again without looking at the paper.

Before you know it, you'll be a tongue twister champion!

Which witch is which?

Shelly shaved six silly sheep.

Toy boat.

Pirates' private property.

Peppered pickles.

Willie's really weary.

Silly superstition.

Right ring, wrong ring.

Eddie edited it.

Six sticky skeletons.

Black back bat.

Rolling red wagons.

She sees cheese.

Quizzical quiz,
kiss me quick.

Cheryl shares
sticky stickers.

Red leather, yellow leather.

Thin sticks, thick brick.

Starred shards of stars.

Pre-shrunk silk shirts.

Sticky tacky cotton candy.

Box of mixed biscuits.

Good blood, bad blood.

Clowns grow
glowing crowns.

When ripe, wipe clean.

Withering weeping
willow tree.

The sushi chef wears
silver socks.

A cement mixer
mixes cement.

Silly Stat: What do all tongue twisters have in common? When certain combinations of sounds are spoken quickly, the speaker loses control of their mouth. The sounds change to mimic each other, for example, "top cop" changes to "top top," and "toy boat" becomes "toy boyt."

Scissors sizzle,
thistles sizzle.

Sheri's horse
houses horseradish.

He threw three free
throws.

Silly Stat: Do you know the human tongue has eight different muscles?

Rubber baby
buggy bumpers.

A big black bear sat on a big black rug.

Tie twine to
three tree twigs.

Tom threw Tim
three thumbtacks.

I eat eel while you peel eel.

Four fine fresh
fish for you.

Eleven benevolent
elephants.

Nine nice night nurses
nursing nicely.

I thought, I thought of
thinking of thanking you.

She sews silvery sweaters
so well.

The queen in
green screamed.

Seth from Sainsbury's
sells thick socks.

Seven slick slimy snakes
slowly sliding southward.

Silly Stat: Did you know that snakes don't have eyelids? They have a single scale over their eye, so it looks like they sleep with their eyes open!

A savvy sailor swiftly
sailed his ship into a
slippery slip.

Four frenzied friends
flipped through
their phones.

Double bubble gum,
bubbles double.

The white wagon's round
wonky wheels.

Five frantic frogs fled
from fifty fierce fish.

Roofs of mushrooms rarely
mush too much.

Round and round
the rugged rocks
the ragged rascal ran.

Wayne went to Wales
to watch walruses.

Roberta ran rings around
the Roman ruins.

Six sleek swans swam
swiftly southward.

Silly Stat: Did you know
a male swan is called a
"cob," and a female swan
is called a "pen"?

Clean clams crammed
in clean cans.

I scream, you scream,
we all scream for
ice cream!

Can you can a can as a
canner can can a can?

Andy and Andi-Ann's
anniversary is in April.

I saw a kitten eating
chicken in the kitchen.

Near an ear, a nearer ear,
a nearly eerie ear.

Which wristwatches are
Swiss wristwatches?

I'd rather lather with
lavender soap.

If a dog chews shoes, whose
shoes does he choose?

A sliver of slithering
snake scales.

Don't give crunchy
potato chips to touchy
chinchillas.

Silly Stat: Did you know
it takes four pounds of
raw potatoes to make one
pound of potato chips?

How many saws could a
seesaw saw if a seesaw
could saw saws?

Fuzzy Wuzzy was a bear.
Fuzzy Wuzzy had no hair.
Fuzzy Wuzzy wasn't fuzzy,
was he?

I have got a date at a quarter to eight. I'll see you at the gate, so don't be late.

As one blue bug bled black blood the other black bug bled blue.

Thirty-three thirsty, thundering thoroughbreds thumped Mr. Thurber on Thursday.

One-One was a racehorse. Two-Two was one, too. When One-One won one race, Two-two won one, too.

How much wood would a woodchuck chuck if a woodchuck could chuck wood? As much wood as a woodchuck would if a woodchuck could chuck wood.

She sells seashells by the seashore. And the shells she sells by the seashore are seashells for sure.

Silly Stat: The story behind "She Sells Seashells" is famous. It is said the rhyme is about the 19th-century English paleontologist Mary Anning. Mary was the first female fossil hunter thought to have first discovered dinosaur bones! She also identified fossilized dinosaur poop.

Peter Piper picked a peck of pickled peppers. A peck of pickled peppers Peter Piper picked. If Peter Piper picked a peck of pickled peppers, where's the peck of pickled peppers that Peter Piper picked?

Silly Stat: Peter and his famous pickled peppers first appeared in print in 1813 in John Harris's *Peter Piper's Practical Principles of Plain and Perfect Pronunciation.*

Betty Botter bought some butter. But she said the butter's bitter. If I put it in my batter, it will make my batter bitter. But a bit of bitter butter will make my batter better. So 'twas better Betty Botter bought a bit of bitter butter.

There was a fisherman named Fisher, who fished for some fish in a fissure. 'Til a fish with a grin, pulled the fisherman in. Now they're fishing the fissure for Fisher.

Chester cheetah chews a chunk of cheap Cheddar cheese. If the chunk of cheap Cheddar cheese chunked Chester cheetah, what would Chester cheetah chew on?

Silly Stat: According to researchers at the Massachusetts Institute of Technology (MIT), this is the hardest tongue twister: "Pad kid poured curd pulled cod." According to Guinness World Records, this is the most difficult tongue twister: "The sixth sick sheikh's sixth sheep's sick." Which one gets your vote as the toughest tongue twister?

How many berries could a bare berry carry, if a bare berry could carry berries? Well they can't carry berries (which could make you very wary), but a bare berry carried is more scary!

Silly Sally swiftly shooed seven silly sheep. The seven silly sheep Silly Sally shooed shilly-shallied south.

How much caramel can a cannonball cram in a camel if a cannonball can cram caramel in a camel?

All I want is a proper cup of coffee made in a proper copper coffeepot. I may be off my dot, but I want a cup of coffee from a proper coffeepot. Tin coffeepots and iron coffeepots, they're no use to me. If I can't have a proper cup of coffee in a proper copper coffeepot, I'll have a cup of tea.

I thought a thought. But the thought I thought wasn't the thought I thought I thought. If the thought I thought I thought had been the thought I thought, I wouldn't have thought so much.

Tessie tasted toasty toast, so she could test the toaster. The toaster took toast and toasted it till it was toasty toast.

As he gobbled the cakes on his plate, the greedy ape said as he ate, "The greener green grapes are, the keener keen apes are to gobble green grape cakes, they're great!"

How many cans can a cannibal nibble if a cannibal can nibble cans? As many cans as a cannibal can nibble if a cannibal can nibble cans.

Granny Green grins greatly, gearing up to go gallivanting. Gallivanting gear waits for Granny where she wears her grin.

A tutor who tooted the flute tried to tutor two tooters to toot. Said the two to the tutor, "Is it tougher to toot or to tutor two tooters to toot?"

How much ground would a groundhog hog, if a groundhog could hog ground? A groundhog would hog all the ground he could hog if a groundhog could hog ground.

Through three cheese trees three free fleas flew. While these fleas flew, freezy breeze blew. Freezy breeze made these three trees freeze. Freezy trees made these trees' cheese freeze. That's what made these three free fleas sneeze.

Sheila shares seven shakes with shiny shelled snails
resting on several swaying squashed squares.

How many cookies could a good cook cook, if a good cook could cook cookies? A good cook could cook as many cookies as a good cook who could cook cookies.

> **Silly Stat:** Many sounds use the same muscles, like "c" and "g," or "r" and "w." If you have trouble saying words like "cup" or "cookie," you will probably have trouble with words like "good" and "going."

Of all the felt I ever felt, I never felt a piece of felt which felt as fine as that felt felt when first I felt that felt hat's felt.

It's fun to run with a pun on the tongue, but the tongue doesn't know how to run. So the pun has to run until it is done, so the tongue doesn't have any fun.

4

PUNS

Puns are another kind of joke that juggles word meaning. Sometimes, two words are spelled the same, but the pun plays with their different definitions. Take this one: Broken pencils are pretty *pointless*. Can you think of two meanings for the word "pointless"?

Other times, puns play with words that sound similar but have different meanings, like this: Haunted French pancakes give me the *crepes*. What we really mean is that the haunted French pancake gives us the creeps—yikes! It is funny because crepes are French pancakes.

Puns are clever and they make us think. The more puns you play with, the easier it will be to spot double meanings. In fact, every time you spot a pun, you build on your own *punderful* superpower! Now for some *punny* business . . .

WHEN DO TRUCK DRIVERS STOP TO EAT?

WHENEVER THEY COME TO A *fork* IN THE ROAD.

Every calendar's days are **numbered**.

Silly Stat: In San Juan Chamula, Mexico, a traditional verbal contest called "k'ehel k'op" dates back to Mayan times. Contestants would rap out puns and see who could creatively out-pun the other.

I tried to catch some fog, but I **mist**.

Velcro—**what a rip off**!

I call my horse Mayo, and sometimes Mayo **neighs**.

Two silk worms had a race. They ended up in a **tie**.

A golf ball is a golf ball no matter how you **putt** it.

Be kind to your dentist; he has **fillings,** too.

Why was Cinderella cut from the soccer team? She ran away from the **ball**.

Venison for dinner again? Oh, **deer**!

Time flies like an arrow. Fruit flies **like** banana.

You can lead a horse to water, but a pencil must be **lead**.

A bicycle can't stand on its own because it is **two-tired**.

I didn't like my beard at first, then it **grew on me**.

Reading while sunbathing makes you well **red**.

Did you hear the joke about peanut butter? I'm not **spreading** it.

A dog had puppies near the road and was ticketed for **littering**.

I did a theatrical performance about puns. It was a **play on words**.

Silly Stat: William Shakespeare, Charles Dickens, Oscar Wilde, and Peggy Parish all liked to use puns in their work. In fact, Shakespeare was a fan of poop puns!

All the toilets in New York's police stations have been stolen. Police have **nothing to go on**.

I used to be a banker, but then I lost **interest**.

I can't believe I got fired from the calendar factory. All I did was take a **day off**.

No matter how much you push the envelope, it'll still be **stationery**.

I thought about becoming a witch, so I tried it for a **spell**.

Broken puppets for sale, **no strings attached**.

Those new corduroy pillows are making **headlines**.

Did you hear about the seafood diet? Every time you **see food,** you eat it!

I was going to look for my missing watch, but I could never **find the time**.

I asked my dad to make me a pair of pants. He was happy to, or at least, **sew it seams**.

Once you've seen one shopping center you've **seen a mall**.

Getting paid to sleep would be a **dream job**.

My fear of moving stairs is **escalating**.

Do cannibals like to **meat** people?

I don't trust these stairs. They're always **up to something**.

Parmesan cheese is **grate** for you.

Two hats were hanging on a hat rack in the hallway. One hat said to the other, "You stay here; I'll go on **a head**."

A book just fell on my head. I've only got **my shelf** to blame.

When tortilla chips don't sell fast enough, the maker knows it will soon be **crunch** time.

Silly Stat: When there are pun competitions, punslingers compete in rapid-fire duels for the title. They get a total of five seconds to come up with their pun. Whoever runs out of time or has three strikes first, loses.

To the guy who invented zero: Thanks for **nothing**!

I stayed up all night to see where the sun went, and then it **dawned** on me.

Inspecting mirrors is a job I could really **see myself** doing.

Why couldn't Goldilocks sleep?
Because she had **night-bears**.

Where do sailors take baths?

A *tub-marine*.

What happens when a sea monster gets angry?

It causes a *comm-ocean*.

What do you call a fairy that has not taken a bath?

Stinker Bell.

Silly Stat: Traditional Palestinian weddings have held pun-derful oral poetry duels for hundreds of years.

What did the beach say when the tide finally came in?

Long time, no *sea*.

Why did the pig want to be an actor?

Because he was a real *ham*.

What color socks do bears wear?

They prefer *bare* feet.

What's five thousand miles long and purple?

The *grape* wall of China.

Why isn't your nose twelve inches long?

Because then it would be a *foot*.

How do snails fight?

They *slug* it out.

How do bees get to school?

The school *buzzz*.

Why can't chickens play baseball?

Because they hit *fowl* balls.

What kind of cats like to go bowling?
Alley cats.

Where do butterflies sleep?
On *cater-pillows*.

Silly Stat: Homographic puns have two words that sound different but are spelled the same. Take, for instance, a bass player versus a bass fish.

What do you call a grumpy cow?
Moooo-dy.

What is the strongest creature in the sea?
A *mussel*.

How do you make an orange laugh?
Tickle its *navel*.

Why did the outlaw rob the bakery?
He *kneaded* the dough.

Why did the sheriff go to the barbecue?
He heard it was a place to have a *steak* out.

What do you get when you cross a sea creature and drums?
Fish sticks.

What bird can be heard at mealtimes?
A *swallow*.

What did the doctor prescribe to the sick lemon?
Lemon-*aid*.

How do you invite a dinosaur for lunch?
Tea, Rex?

What do you call a kitten
who has sprouted fins
and loves to swim?

A *catfish*.

What is the craziest,
wackiest, most
bizarre fruit?

Coconut.

A skeleton walks into a
restaurant and places
an order for lunch.
What is his order?

Spare *ribs*.

What is the musical
part of a snake?

The *scales*.

When is music
like vegetables?

When you dance
to the *beet*.

What does a clock do
when it's hungry?

It goes back *four seconds*.

What fruit never ever
wants to be alone?

A *pear*.

Where did the music
teacher leave his keys?

On the *piano*.

Silly Stat: The English
language was made for
puns. The Oxford Dictionary
estimates that there are
250,000-plus words in
the English language
to have *pun* with!

What do you call an owl
that does magic tricks?

Hoo-dini.

What do baseball
players eat on?

Home *plates*.

How do turtles talk to each other?
By using *shell* phones.

What did the person who invented the door knocker win?

The No-*bell* prize.

What do you call an academically successful piece of bread?

An honor *roll*.

What do you call a pod of musical whales?

An *orca*-stra.

How did dinosaurs decorate their bathrooms?

With rep*tiles*.

Silly Stat: Nobel Prize winners are called "laureates," after the Greek laurel wreath given to the best competitors in the olden days. Famous Nobel Prize winners include former U.S. President Barack Obama, who received the Nobel Peace Prize in 2009, and musician Bob Dylan, who received the Nobel Prize in Literature in 2016.

What do they call a school with a door made of iron?

The school of *hard knocks*.

How do you know it was an emotional wedding?

The cake was in *tiers*.

What happened to the train driver when he retired?

He got *sidetracked*.

Silly Stat: Every year Austin, Texas hosts the O. Henry Pun-Off World Championships—the most prestigious pun competition in the United States. One lucky winner goes home with the POTY or Punster of the Year Award.

What happened to the guy who got hit in the head with a soda can?

He was lucky it was a *soft* drink.

What happened to the kid who accidentally swallowed some Scrabble tiles?

His next poop could *spell* disaster.

Why do potatoes make good detectives?

Because they keep their *eyes peeled*.

Some guy just threw milk and cheese at me.

How *dairy*!

What do you call a runaway pea?

An *esca-pea*.

What do you call a lazy spud?

A *couch potato*.

What do you call a dinosaur at the rodeo?

A *bronco*-saurus.

Why do magicians do so well in school?

They're good at *trick* questions.

Two vegetarians got into an argument.

Do they still have a *beef* with each other?

What happened when my friend told me he was turning vegan?

I said, "That's a big *missed steak*."

Why did the guy bring a donkey home?

Because he thought he might get a *kick out of it*.

What happened when I didn't understand math?

My teacher *summed* it up.

What was the reporter doing at the ice cream shop?

Getting the *scoop*.

Silly Stat: The word "scoop" is used by reporters when they publish an important news story before anyone else. Clare Hollingworth, an English journalist, was the first reporter to break the story about World War II. This was described as "the scoop of the century."

What happened when I asked the butcher for top-shelf meat?

He said the *steaks were too high*.

What do you call the father of all sodas?

Pop.

How do sales people approach dinosaurs in clothes shops?

Try, sir, a top?

What happens to children who don't pass their coloring exams?

They need a shoulder to *crayon*.

Why did the spider go to the computer?
To check his *website*.

What happened when I decided I was going to grow some herbs?

I couldn't find the *thyme*.

What do you get from a pampered cow?

Spoiled milk.

What do you call Dracula with hay fever?

The Pollen *Count*.

Why shouldn't you lie to an X-ray technician?

They can *see right through* you.

What happens when you sing in the shower and get shampoo in your mouth?

It becomes a *soap opera*.

What happened when the class clown held the door open for me?

I thought it was a nice *jester*.

Silly Stat: Today, humans are better punsters than artificial intelligence (AI). A computer cannot string the words together to form a pun, combine words to make longer ones, or turn verbs into nouns. I guess you could say when it comes to puns, computers *sink* when they think, but humans *sync* when they think.

Have you ever tried to eat a clock?

It's very *time consuming*.

Where do polar bears vote?

The North *Pole*.

Did you hear about the guy whose whole left side was cut off?

He's all *right* now.

Why are playing cards like wolves?
They come in *packs*.

Why did I burn my Hawaiian pizza today?

I think I should have cooked it on *aloha* temperature.

What do you call a knight who is afraid to fight?

Sir Render.

How do you fix a broken tomato?

With tomato *paste*.

Why are fish so smart?

Because they live in *schools*.

What do you get if you cross a snake and a LEGO set?

A boa *constructor*.

Silly Stat: The origin of the word "surrender" is French and it means to give up. The French famously surrendered during the Battle of Agincourt on October 25, 1415, against the English.

5

RIDDLES

Riddles are funny word puzzles that use imagination and humor to solve a problem. When approaching a riddle, be sure to pay close attention to the clues. Remember, you already have all the information you need to figure it out. Have confidence!

Let's try one: I am an odd number. Take away one letter and I become even. What number am I?

All you need to do is look at the sentence from a new angle. Think of the first ten numbers. We can eliminate half of them right away with the information that they are even. That leaves us with, one, three, five, seven, and nine.

Do you see the word "even" in any of these words? If you remove the "s" from seven, what do you have left? The word "even"! You've solved the riddle.

Now you're ready for more riddle detective work . . .

**What tells the time but
needs no winding?**

A ROOSTER.

What has to be broken
before you can use it?

An egg.

What has hands but
doesn't clap?

A clock.

If a red house is made
of red bricks, and a
yellow house is made of
yellow bricks, what is a
greenhouse made of?

Glass.

What is so fragile that
saying its name breaks it?

Silence.

What goes up but never
comes back down?

Your age.

Zachary's parents
have three sons:
Snap, Crackle, and . . . ?

Zachary.

There are two monkeys
on a tree and one jumps
off. Why does the other
monkey jump, too?

Monkey see, monkey do.

What begins with "t,"
finishes with "t,"
and has tea in it?

A teapot.

You bring me for
dinner but never eat
me, what am I?

A knife and fork.

What has four *i*'s
but can't see?

Mississippi.

What is orange and
sounds like a parrot?

A carrot.

What is easy to get into
but hard to get out of?

Trouble.

What is full of holes but still holds water?

A sponge.

If a father, mother, and their children weren't under an umbrella, why didn't they get wet?

It wasn't raining.

You draw a line. Without touching it, how do you make it a longer line?

Draw a short line next to it and now it's the longer line.

Where does success come before work?

The dictionary.

What has green hair, a round red head, and a long, thin white beard?

A radish.

Where can you find cities, towns, shops, and streets but no people?

A map.

Almost everyone needs it, asks for it, gives it, but almost nobody takes it. What is it?

Advice.

What belongs to you but is used more by others?

Your name.

What has a neck but no head?

A bottle.

What starts with a "p," ends with an "e," and has thousands of letters?

The post office.

What comes once in a minute, twice in a moment, but never in a thousand years?

The letter "m."

What question can you never answer "yes" to?

"Are you asleep?"

I have no feet, no hands, no wings, but I climb the sky. What am I?

Smoke.

Three men were in a boat. It capsized, but only two got their hair wet. Why?

One was bald.

Eric throws a ball as hard as he can. It comes back to him, even though nothing and nobody has touched it. How?

He throws it straight up in the air.

If an electric train is traveling south, which way is the smoke going?

There is no smoke—it is an electric train.

What is next in this sequence? JFMAMJJASON . . .

The letter "D." The sequence contains the first letter of each month.

What is shaped like a box, has no feet, and runs up and down?

An elevator.

What asks no questions but requires many answers?

A doorbell.

How do you spell enemy in three letters?

F-O-E.

Silly Stat: One of Batman's most famous enemies in the comics is The Riddler. His real name is Edward Nygma. Get it?

While looking at a photograph, a man said, "Brothers and sisters have I none. That man's father is my father's son." Who was the person in the photograph?

The man's son.

When is the best time to have lunch?

After breakfast.

How far is it from March to June?

A single spring.

What goes up and down but never moves?

The temperature.

You go into the woods to get it. Then you sit down to find it. Then you go home because you couldn't find it. What am I?

A splinter.

A queen bee was buzzing, a worker bee was buzzing, a honey bee was buzzing, and a killer bee was buzzing. How many *b*'s are in buzzing?

One. There is only one "b" in "buzzing."

I can run but not walk. Wherever I go, thought follows me close behind. What am I?

A nose.

Why should you always carry a watch when crossing a desert?

It has a spring in it.

With what two animals do most people go to bed?

Two calves.

What has a tongue, but never talks—has no legs, but sometimes walks?

A shoe.

When is a bump like a hat?

When it is felt.

What is yellow, looks like a crescent moon, and has seeds?

A banana.

**The more I appear,
the less you see.
What is it I could be?**

Darkness.

When is a door not a door?

When it's ajar.

What is the oldest tree?

The elder.

**I'm a container without
hinges, a key, or a lid,
yet golden treasure is
inside. What am I?**

An egg.

**What is the best thing
to put into pies?**

Your teeth.

**I am always in front of
you, but you will never
see me. What am I?**

The future.

**When is a man
like a snake?**

When he's rattled.

**What has teeth but doesn't
use them for eating?**

A comb.

**What is the difference
between the North Pole
and the South Pole?**

The world.

**If snakes marry, what
might their towels say?**

Hissss and hers.

**What is the last thing
you take off before bed?**

Your feet off the floor.

**What invention lets you
look right through a wall?**

A window.

**Name three days
consecutively where
none of the seven days
of the week appear.**

Yesterday, today,
and tomorrow.

A man was driving a black truck. His lights were not on. The moon was not out. A lady was crossing the street. How did the man see her?

It was a bright, sunny day.

A doctor and a boy were fishing. The boy was the doctor's son, but the doctor was not the boy's father. Who was the doctor?

His mother.

How do you make the number one disappear?

Add the letter "g" and it's "gone."

What bank never has any money?

The riverbank.

Ms. Blue lives in the blue house, Mr. Pink lives in the pink house, and Mr. Brown lives in the brown house. Who lives in the White House?

The U.S. president.

If you threw a white stone into the Red Sea, what would it become?

Wet.

What has four legs, but can't walk?

A table.

In a one-story pink house, there was a pink person, a pink cat, a pink fish, a pink computer, a pink chair, a pink table, a pink telephone, a pink shower—everything was pink! What color were the stairs?

There are no stairs. It's a one-story house.

I have keys but no locks. I have space but no room. You can enter but can't go outside. What am I?

A computer keyboard.

How do you spell "cow" in 11 letters?

SEE-O-DOUBLE-U.

I am not alive, but I grow. I've got no lungs, but I need air.
I don't have a mouth, but water drowns me. What am I?

Fire.

What animal grows down as it grows up?

A goose.

How far can a fox run into the woods?

Only halfway, otherwise it would be running out of the woods.

What is bought by the yard and worn by the foot?

Carpet.

I make a loud noise when I am changing. I get lighter as I get bigger. What am I?

Popcorn.

What does a cat have that no other animal has?

Kittens.

I can be any color you can imagine. You see me in everyday life. I've been around for many years. If you look around you can probably see some of me right now. What am I?

Paint.

A monkey, a squirrel, and a bird are racing to the top of a coconut tree. Who will get the banana first?

None of them. You can't get a banana from a coconut tree!

I am a number with a couple of friends; quarter a dozen, and you'll find me again. What am I?

Three.

Silly Stat: The word dozen means a group of 12. A "baker's dozen" means one more than the standard 12. So, when you buy bagels, ask for a baker's dozen and you'll get 13!

If there are four apples and you take away three, how many do you have?

You took three apples, so you have three.

How many times can you subtract the number five from 25?

Once, because after you've subtracted five, it's no longer the number 25.

Which month has 28 days?

All of them, of course!

If two's company and three's a crowd, what are four and five?

Nine.

What has a thumb and four fingers, but is not alive?

A glove.

What's the easiest way to double your money?

Fold it in half.

When you have me, you feel like sharing me. But if you share me you don't have me. What am I?

A secret.

What weighs more, a pound of iron or a pound of feathers?

Both would weigh the same. A pound is a pound.

If a rooster laid 13 eggs and the farmer took eight of them and then another rooster laid 12 eggs and four of them were rotten, how many of the eggs were left?

Roosters don't lay eggs.

Two fathers and two sons sat down to eat eggs for breakfast. They ate exactly three eggs, each person had an egg. Explain how they did it.

One of the fathers is also a grandfather. Therefore, one father is both a son and a father. That makes three people, so each got an egg.

Laura has four daughters, each of her daughters has a brother, how many children does Laura have?

Five, each daughter has the same brother.

What tastes better than it smells?

A tongue.

How many letters are there in the English alphabet?

18: three in "the," seven in "English," and eight in "alphabet."

Throw away the outside and cook the inside, then eat the outside, and throw away the inside. What is it?

Corn on the cob. You throw away the husk, cook and eat the kernels, and throw away the cob.

Take off my skin, I won't cry, but you will. What am I?

An onion.

How can a leopard change its spots?

By moving from one spot to another.

I am a seed with three letters in my name. Take away two letters and I sound quite the same. What am I?

A pea.

I am a bird, I am a fruit, and I am a person. What am I?

A Kiwi.

A one-seeded fruit I may be, but all of your calendars are full of me. What am I?

Dates.

I have wings and I have a tail, across the sky is where I sail. Yet I have no eyes, ears, or mouth. What am I?

A kite.

She's the head of a hive. On a chessboard, she is seen. She's in a deck of cards. Who could she be?

A queen.

It is there from the very start and will be there until the end. To end you must cross over. And you must pass through it to begin.

The finish line.

I go around and round, with no beginning and no end. What am I?

A doughnut.

Your mother and father have a child. It's not your brother and not your sister. Who is it?

You.

What is often on the ground getting stepped on by others, but you don't have to wash it because it never gets dirty; in fact, you couldn't wash it even if you tried?

A shadow.

I am beautiful, up in the sky. I am magical, yet I cannot fly. To some people, I bring luck; to some people, riches. The person at my end does whatever he wishes. What am I?

A rainbow.

Reaching stiffly for the sky, I bare my fingers when it's cold. In warmth, I wear an emerald glove and in between, I dress in gold. What am I?

A tree.

What lives without a body, hears without ears, speaks without a mouth, to which the air alone gives birth?

An echo.

My feet stay warm, but my head is cold. No one can move me, I'm just too old. What am I?

A mountain.

Built of metal or wood to divide. It will make us good neighbors, if you stay on your side. What is it?

A fence.

6

WAIT FOR IT . . .

Welcome to jokes with a longer setup. How do longer jokes work?

Read the stories below and make them yours. Take the time to learn them, so you can tell them as if they happened to you. Remember to pace yourself so your audience eagerly anticipates the punchline. Have them perched on the edge of their seats, then . . . deliver it!

Use longer jokes around the campfire, at home, in the car, or whenever you feel like telling a story or taking the stage!

A DUCK WADDLES INTO THE GROCERY STORE TO BUY A CAN OF SODA. THE CLERK LOOKS DOWN AT HIM AND ASKS, "WOULD YOU LIKE TO PAY WITH CASH OR CREDIT?" THE DUCK REPLIES, "JUST PUT IT ON MY BILL."

David is hungry and stops at the local restaurant for a bowl of soup. The waiter brings it over and places it on the table in front of him. David's stomach rumbles with hunger. He picks up his spoon, excited to take his first bite, when he freezes. Nestled among the tasty noodles is a fly. "Waiter!" he calls. The waiter rushes over. "Yes?" "What is this fly doing in my soup?" The waiter leans over, his nose almost touching the bowl, and replies, "The backstroke."

Two fleas go to the movies. When they get out, they stand for a while in the traffic. All around them people are rushing, horns are blaring. One flea turns to the other and asks, "Do you want to walk or should we take a dog home?"

Two knives are side by side in the silverware drawer. One knife turns to the other and says, "You're looking sharp!"

Jason stands nervously before the teacher. "Would I get in trouble for something I didn't do?" Mrs. Roberts replies, "Of course not." "Good," Jason says. "Because I didn't do my homework."

A young boy knocks on the door on Halloween night and says, "Trick or treat?" The woman opens the door and looks at him. After a few seconds, she says, "I don't know if I can give you a treat. What are you supposed to be?" "A werewolf," the boy answers. The woman shakes her head. "But you're not wearing a costume. You've only got your normal clothes on." With a laugh, the boy replies, "Well, it's not a full moon yet, is it?"

Alex looks very sad, so his friend Saeed asks him what is wrong. "I lost my dog today," Alex says. Saeed nods, "That's too bad. Hey, why don't you put an ad in the paper?" Alex thinks about it for a bit then shakes his head. "What good would that do? My dog can't read."

A boy asks his father, "Dad, are bugs good to eat?" "Son, please don't talk about things like that over dinner," the dad replies. After dinner the father asks, "Now, son, what did you want to ask me?" "Oh, nothing," the boy says. "There was a bug in your soup, but you ate it."

The teacher says to the class, "A man rode his horse to town on Friday. The very next day he rode back on Friday. How is this possible?" Keisha raises her hand and says, "The horse's name was Friday."

"Yuki, why is your little sister crying?" Mom asks her son, while watching her daughter sob with dismay. Yuki shrugs and replies, "Because I helped her." Mom relaxes back into her seat with a relieved smile. "But that's a good thing! What did you help her with?" she asks proudly as her daughter wails loudly. Yuki says, "I helped her eat the rest of her gummy bears."

"I'm the fastest animal in the jungle," the lion roars. The cheetah shakes her head. "I don't think so. Let's race and see." The whole population of the jungle shows up. Elephants stand next to gazelles. Rhinos and hippos line up. Hyenas and zebras and every other animal wait to see the outcome of the race. The lion is very confident he will win. The race begins and the cheetah takes off. She wins by a mile and is declared the fastest animal in the jungle. The lion is embarrassed and can't believe he lost. "You're a cheater!" he shouts. "Yep, and you're a lion," the cheetah replies.

Jennifer goes to visit her friend and is amazed to find her playing chess with her dog. The little Shih Tzu sits on a cushion, and Jennifer watches with fascination as the dog's little front paw accurately moves the pieces around the board. "I can hardly believe my eyes!" Jennifer exclaims in astonishment. Her friend waves her hand in dismissal. "Oh, she's not so smart. I've beaten her three games out of five."

A bear walks into a coffee shop and tells the barista, "I'll have a latte . . . . with extra foam." The barista replies, "What's with the big pause?" The bear looks at his paws and replies, "I don't know, my dad has them, too."

Arjun holds up his smartphone. "I had to take my phone to the dentist yesterday." "Really, why?" says Gabi. Arjun answers, "Because it had a Bluetooth."

"Jada, why can't dinosaurs clap?" Jada thinks for a minute and says, "Because they're extinct!"

Mr. Noah goes in for a very special surgery on his hands. The doctor tells him how complicated it will be. Mr. Noah holds up his hands and says, "Doctor, will I be able to play piano once you are done?" The doctor nods. "Of course!" "That's good," Mr. Noah replies. "Because I've always wanted to play the piano."

Diego walks up to his mother and says, "Mom, all the kids at school make fun of me." His mother asks, "Why, sweetie?" Diego replies, "Well, Mom, all the other students say I'm a werewolf." She pats him on the head and says, "Don't worry honey, just remember at nighttime to comb all your fur to the right side."

Elijah sits glumly on the porch, his hand holding his chin. Stuart rides by on his bike and sees his friend deep in thought. He jumps off and puts his bike against the fence. "Hey, Elijah. What's bothering you, buddy?" "Oh, I heard a funny joke about a boomerang earlier, and I've forgotten it." "Don't worry about it," Stuart tells him. "I'm sure it will come back to you eventually."

I like Northern and Eastern European food, so I decided to Russia over there because I was Hungary. After Czeching the menu, I ordered Turkey, with a Danish. When I was Finnished, I told the waiter, "It's all good, but there is Norway I could eat another bite."

David goes back the next day. He gets the same waiter and again looks down into his bowl of soup and sees another fly! "Waiter," he cries out. "There's another fly in my soup." The waiter walks over to peer down. He looks at the rest of the table and says, "Don't worry, sir, the spider from the bread roll will get him."

David has just about had it with this restaurant, but he gives it one last try. "Waiter," he asks. "Can I have cold mashed potatoes, burnt chicken, and a wilted salad?" The waiter gives him a funny look and replies, "No, we don't serve food like that here." David smiles and says, "You did the last time I was here."

A man gets his house painted. When the painters are finished, they hand him the bill. He is surprised to find that the painters have not charged him for paint, just for painting. He asks them, "You did a great job, but why didn't you charge me for paint, too?" The painter replies, "Don't worry about the paint, sir. It's on the house."

An ant and a centipede are hanging out and having a great time. After an hour or so, they run out of food. The ant decides to go out and get more, but the centipede tells him, "Let me go, I'm faster with all of my legs." The ant says, "You're right about that. Okay, you go." The ant waits and waits. After a couple of hours, he wonders where the centipede is, and calls. "What's taking so long?" he asks impatiently. The centipede replies, "Hold on, I almost have all my shoes on."

Finding one of his students making faces at others on the playground, Mr. Mason stops to gently reprimand the child. Smiling kindly, the teacher says, "Johnny, when I was a little boy, I was told that if I made faces, my face would freeze like that." Little Johnny looks up and replies, "Well, Mr. Mason, you can't say you weren't warned."

Mr. P. doesn't like to spend money, but his wife and daughter convince him to go out for dinner. He reluctantly agrees to go to a local restaurant. When he enters the restaurant, he asks the host, "How are your prices?" The host replies, looking at the man's daughter, "Well, kids eat free." Mr. P. replies, "In that case, my daughter is really hungry. She's going to have three plates."

Gabe is sitting at home when he hears a knock at the door. He opens the door and sees a tiny snail on the porch. He picks up the snail and throws it as far as he can. A year later, there's a knock at the door. Gabe opens it and sees the same snail. The snail looks up at him and says, "What was that all about, man?"

On a hot day in August, a mailman pauses by an old house where a painter is busy painting it from top to bottom. The painter is dripping with sweat. He is wearing a heavy parka as if it were the middle of the winter. The postman walks up to the mailbox, and to his surprise, he realizes the painter has another jacket on underneath the opened parka. The puzzled mailman says, "It's kind of hot today." "Sure is," says the painter, who pauses to take a long drink of water and wipe his brow. The mailman points to the painter. "Why are you wearing those parkas, then?" The painter holds up the paint can he is using and shows the mailman the instructions. "Says right here, 'For best results, put on two coats.'"

Kayla goes with her dad to pick up fruit and vegetables at a local farm. It is hot outside and she notices a boy scratching his foot in the dirt. He bobs his head and says, "Cluck, cluck, cluck." Kayla jumps back in shock. "Why is that boy saying, 'Cluck, cluck, cluck,' and scratching in the dirt?" The mother of the boy is stocking produce in the bins. "Oh, he thinks he's a chicken." Kayla shakes her head. "Well, why don't you tell him he's not a chicken?" The boy's mother looks around to see if anybody is listening. She leans closer to Kayla and whispers, "Well, we need the eggs."

A woman is driving a truck down the road when a policeman hails her down. In the rear of the truck are a gaggle of penguins. The policeman walks up to the truck and asks, "What are you doing with all these penguins?" "These are my penguins," the woman replies. "They belong to me." "You need to take them to a zoo," the policeman insists. The driver nods and says, "Will do." The next day, at the same time, and at the same intersection, the policeman sees the truck filled with penguins. He halts the driver and says, "I thought I told you to take these penguins to the zoo." The woman nods. "I did," she says calmly. "And today, I'm taking them to the movies."

Three friends are stranded on a desert island. All they want is to go home, but no ships have passed by and they are quite alone in the middle of nowhere. One day, one of them digs a hole and, to his surprise, pulls out a lamp. "Maybe it's a magic lamp. Rub it and let's see if a genie appears!" one of the men shouts. The man who found it gently wipes the grit from the lamp and, to his astonishment, smoke pours from the spout to curl around their heads. "Holy cow! That's a real genie," he cries. "Yes," the deep voice fills the air. "I will grant you three wishes. Remember to use them wisely. There will be only three wishes allowed." One of the friends rushes forward and shouts, "I want to go home, now!" The genie snaps his fingers and the first friend vanishes in a puff of purple smoke. "I want to go home, too," the second friend proclaims. In an instant, he, too, is gone. The third man looks at the empty island and the blue expanse of the sea. He hears nothing but the cry of the seagulls and the crash of the waves. He swallows a sob and says, "I sure am lonely. I wish I had my friends back."

Grandpa is very grumpy. He stomps around the house with a scowl on his face. "Gramps," his granddaughter asks. "Is your foot bothering you?" He shakes his head, "Nah. Gout is under control right now." "Don't you like your new cane?" "What, this thing?" He holds up the walking stick. "It's fine." "Then what is it?" Grandpa sighs and points to the steps going upstairs. "It's the chairlift your father installed—the darn thing is driving me up a wall!"

Robert breaks both of his arms in an accident, so he has to wear a cast on each arm from wrist to elbow. Eventually, with his two casts, he takes a walk and pauses outside of a music shop. In the window is the most beautiful guitar he has ever seen. He stares at it for a long time, shakes his head, and walks through the door. "How much is that guitar?" He nods toward the instrument. "That one? It's very expensive," the owner responds. "I don't care! I'm going to buy it." The owner looks at the guitar and at Robert's two casts. "How will you use it?" Robert smiles. "I'll just play it by ear."

A kangaroo and rabbit are sitting together in the brush watching their offspring. "Oh, no," the kangaroo moans. "What's wrong?" The rabbit pauses from eating her carrot. "It's the forecast. It's calling for rain." The rabbit sniffs the air a bit. "That's okay. We could use the water." "Sure." The kangaroo pats her pouch. "But that means my kids will have to play inside all day."

One day a man with an elephant walks into a movie theater. "I'm afraid I can't let your elephant in here, sir," the manager says. "Oh, don't worry. He's very well behaved," the man says. "All right, then," the manager says. "If you're sure . . ." After the movie, the manager says to the man, "I'm very surprised! Your elephant was so well behaved, and he even seemed to enjoy the movie!" "Yes, I was surprised, too," says the man. "Especially since he wasn't a fan of the book."

A chicken marches into the library, walks up to the library desk and says, "Book, book, BOOK!" The librarian hands over a couple of thin paperbacks and watches the chicken leave the library, walk across the street, through a field, and disappear down a hill. The next day, the chicken is back. It walks right up to the librarian, drops the books on her desk, and says, "Book, Book, BOOK, BOOK!" The librarian hands over a few more books and watches the chicken drag them away. The next day, the chicken comes for a third time, and once again goes through the same routine. This time, once the chicken is out the door, the librarian follows—across the street, through a field, and down the hill to a small pond. On a rock at the edge of the pond is the biggest frog the librarian has ever seen. The chicken walks up to the frog, drops the book on the pond's edge, and says, "Book, Book, Book!" The frog hops over, uses its front leg to push through the pile, and says: "Read it, read it, read it."

Four boys were late for school, so the teacher asks one of them, "Ryan, why were you late?" Ryan responds, "Because, my clock was 15 minutes late." Next the teacher asks, "Garrett, why were you late?" Garrett answers, "Because my tires were flat." The teacher then asks, "Scott, why were you late?" Scott belches and says, "I ate too much this morning, so I walked slowly to school." After Scott finishes, Jack starts to cry. The teacher asks, "Why are you crying, Jack? I didn't even ask you yet." Jack replies, "They used up all my excuses."

Howie visits his 90-year-old grandpa who lives way out in the country. On the first morning of the visit, Howie's grandpa prepares a breakfast of bacon and eggs. Howie notices a filmy substance on his plate and asks, "Are these plates clean, Gramps?" His grandpa replies, "They're as clean as cold water can get them. Just go ahead and finish your meal." For lunch, Grandpa makes hamburgers. Again, Howie is concerned about the plates. His has specks of dried egg on it. "Are you sure these plates are clean?" he asks, flaking off the dried food. Without looking up, Grandpa says, "I told you before, those dishes are as clean as cold water can get them!" Later, as Howie is leaving, his grandpa's dog won't let him pass. Howie says, "Gramps, your dog won't let me walk by him." Grandpa yells to the dog, "Cold Water, go lie down!"

Anton comes running into the house. "Mom, there's a man outside with a broken arm named Sheldon." "Well," says Mom. "That's a funny name for a broken arm!"

A jockey is about to enter a race on a new horse. The horse's trainer meets him before the race and says, "All you have to remember with this horse is that every time you approach a jump, you have to shout, 'ALLLEEEY-OOOP!' really loudly in the horse's ear. As long as you do that, you'll be fine." The jockey thinks the trainer is little bit wacky, but promises to shout those words. The race begins and they approach the first hurdle. The jockey ignores the trainer's silly advice and the horse crashes straight through the center of the jump. They keep going and approach the second hurdle. The jockey, somewhat embarrassed, whispers "Alley-oop" in the horse's ear. The same thing happens—the horse crashes straight through the center of the jump. At the third hurdle, the jockey thinks, "It's no good, I'll have to do it," and yells, "ALLLEEEY-OOOP!" really loudly. Sure enough, the horse sails over the jump with no problem. This continues for the rest of the race, but due to the earlier crashes, the horse only finishes third. The trainer asks the jockey what went wrong. The jockey replies, "Nothing is wrong with me—it's this horse. What, is he deaf or something?" The trainer replies, "Deaf? He's not deaf. He's blind!"

A young boy has a dream of being in a circus. He approaches the manager of the circus and tells him, "I can do the best bird impression you have ever seen." The manager says, "That's nothing special, a lot of people can do bird impressions." The boy turns to him and says, "Okay." Then he flaps his arms and flies away.

Rebecca's teacher asks her, "If I give you two cats, then two more, and two more cats, how many do you have?" Rebecca calls out, "Seven!" The teacher looks at her and asks more slowly, "If I give you two cats, then two more, and two more cats, how many do you have?" Rebecca repeats, "Seven!" Next, the teacher asks, "If I get two cats, then two more, and two more cats, how many would I have?" Rebecca responds, "Six!" "Good job, Rebecca!" To make sure she really understands, the teacher says, "Now, if I give you two cats, then two more, and two more cats, how many do you have?" Rebecca thinks for a second, "Seven." Her teacher says, "Rebecca, where do you keep getting seven cats from?" Rebecca answers, "You keep giving me six cats, and I already have a cat!"

An elderly woman burst into a pet store. "I want to buy a canary, but it's got to be a good singer." The shop owner begins moving a ladder toward a small cage on a shelf about 15 feet up, near the ceiling of the store. "Ma'am, I've been in this business for 40 years and the best singer I've ever heard is in that cage." "Don't think I'm going to pay a pretty penny just because you are climbing that ladder. It's got to be a singer!" By this point, the shopkeeper is coming down the ladder. "Ma'am, this bird is pretty much a canary Justin Bieber." The bird opens its beak and sings a beautiful tune. Awed, the woman murmurs, "Why, he *is* a good singer." She takes a good look at the bird, her eyes narrowed. "Hey, this bird has only got one leg!" The pet store owner replies, "Do you want a singer or a dancer?"

David goes back to that same restaurant, sits at his usual table, and orders the usual—soup. The waiter sets it down in front of him and says, "No fly!" Then he stands back to watch him eat it. But David just sits there. "Is there something wrong?" the waiter asks. "I can't eat this soup," David replies. "Is it too hot?" the waiter asks. "Nope." "Too cold?" David shakes his head. The waiter calls for the owner and the chef, and each goes through the same routine: "Too hot?" "Too cold?" "No, no . . . No, no." Finally, the chef, at his wit's end, says, "Sir, I will taste the soup myself. Where is the spoon?" David says, "Aha!"

A struggling zoo's main attraction, a gorilla, gets sick during their most popular season. They can't afford to lose the gorilla, so they secretly hire one of the employees to be a gorilla in a suit for an extra $200 a week. The gorilla-man quickly becomes even more popular than the original gorilla. After a few months, he gets less popular, so the gorilla-man decides to raise the stakes. He climbs out of his pen and dangles from a tree in the lion exhibit, but he loses his grip and falls. Scared, he begins to yell for help, "Somebody help!" With this, the lion pounces on top of him and whispers, "Quiet, or you'll get us both fired!"

A pirate walks into a bar with an eye patch, a peg leg, and a hook for a hand. The bartender notices his leg. "How did you get that peg leg?" The pirate replies, "It were many years ago. I were walkin' on the deck when a wave swept a shark aboard. The shark bit off me leg!" "Wow," replies the bartender. "What about that hand?" The pirate nods. "It were many years ago. I were walkin' on the deck when a wave swept a killer whale aboard. The whale bit me bloomin' hand off!" "Oh," says the bartender. "How about the eye?" The pirate replies, "It were many years ago. I were walkin' on the deck when a seagull came outta nowhere and pooped in me eye." "And that blinded you?" asked the bartender. "No, 'twas my first day with the hook."

A man walks into a coffee shop with his dog, but the barista says, "You can't bring your dog in here." The man responds, "This is no ordinary dog. You see, my dog can talk. I'll prove it to you. Sparky, what covers trees?" The dog replies, "Bark!" Next, the man asks, "What's on top of a house?" Sparky answers, "Roof!" Finally, the man asks, "Who's your favorite baseball player?" The dog says, "Ruth!" The barista immediately throws them both out. The man says, "Sheesh, what was that guy's problem?" The dog answers, "Maybe he's not a Yankees fan."

A girl walks into a fancy restaurant and says to the owner, "If you give me free food all night, I will entertain your customers and they will spend lots of money on food all night." "Oh yeah?" says the owner. "How are you going to do that?" The girl gets a hamster out of her pocket and puts it on the piano. The hamster runs up and down the keyboard playing the greatest piano music anyone had ever heard. "That's incredible!" says the owner. "Have you got anything else?" The girl gets a parrot out of her other pocket and puts it on top of the piano. The hamster begins to play the piano again and the parrot sings along. Everyone in the restaurant is amazed and stays all night eating and listening to the hamster and parrot. The owner is delighted. "I must have these animals. Will you sell them to me?" he asks. The girl shakes her head. "Will you sell just one then?" asks the owner. "Okay, I'll sell you the parrot for $100," the girl says. The owner of the restaurant is delighted and hands over the money. Another patron standing next to the girl says, "Don't you think that's quite cheap for such a clever parrot?" "Not at all," the girl replies. "The hamster is a ventriloquist!"

A man goes into a pet shop to buy a parrot. The shop owner points to three identical looking parrots on a perch and states, "The parrot on the left costs $1,000." "Why does that parrot cost so much?" asks the man. The owner says, "Well, that parrot knows how to use a computer." The man then asks about the next parrot. "Oh, that one is $1,500. Not only does it know how to use a computer, but it knows how to program." He points to the third bird on the perch. "That one is $5,000." "What can it do?" The owner shrugged, "To be honest, I have never seen it do a thing, but the other two call him 'boss'!"

One day, Josh runs into his friend Carrie. His nose is all swollen. "What happened to your nose?" she asks. "I sniffed a brose," Josh tells her. "There's no *b* in rose!" says Carrie. "There was in this one," he says.

A cruise ship passes by a remote island in the Pacific Ocean. The passengers cluster on the deck to see a bearded man running around and waving his arms wildly. "Captain," one passenger asks, "who is that man over there?" "I have no idea," the captain says, "but he goes nuts every year when we pass him."

A couple is sitting inside by the fire when the radio announcer comes on: "*We are expecting up to a foot of snow tonight, so please make sure you are parked on the even-numbered side of the road.*" The husband goes out and moves their car. The next day, the same thing happens and the announcer comes on: "*We are expecting up to a foot of snow tonight, please make sure you are parked on the odd-numbered side of the road.*" Again, the man goes out and moves the car. A few days later the same thing happens and the announcer says: "*We are expecting up to two feet of snow tonight, please make sure you are parked on the—*" But the power goes out in the middle of the announcement. The husband starts panicking. "Which side do I put our car on?" His wife looks up from her newspaper and replies, "How about we just leave the car in the garage this time?"

The Big Book of Silly Jokes for Kids 2

Carole P. Roman

Illustrations by
Dylan Goldberger

For my kids and grandkids, who never fail to amuse me. Special thanks to Erin and Joe, without whom this book would not have been written.

If you're too busy to

LAUGH,

you are too busy.

— Proverb

Contents

BUCKLE UP...

...and get ready for a barrel of laughs! Just when you thought you couldn't giggle any more, *The Big Book of Silly Jokes for Kids 2* is here with more fun ways to tickle your family and friends.

Perfect for practicing your joke-telling skills, this book is jam-packed with hundreds of riddles, knock-knock jokes, funny stories, and more to help you develop your punny bone. Did I say *punny*? There are puns in here, too! Don't forget to check out the last chapter and learn to write some new jokes of your own. Creating and telling jokes is a great way to introduce yourself to new friends, stretch your brain, and get lost in the silliness of being a kid.

So, cheer up your best friend, make Mom or Dad laugh, surprise Grandpa with a funny story of your own, and—most important—bring people together in the best way possible. Humor is the fastest way to friendship, fun-filled memories, and glee!

1

SILLY Q & A

What do you get when you cross a rabbit with a snake?
A jump rope.

What event do spiders love to attend?
Webbings.

What do snowmen call their kids?
Chill-dren.

Why didn't the girl trust the ocean?
There was something fishy about it.

Why are skeletons happy?
Because nothing gets under their skin.

How do you make an egg roll?
You push it.

What's a boxer's favorite drink?
Punch.

Why was the man running around his bed?
He wanted to catch up on his sleep.

Where do you find Mexico?
On the map.

Why do witches ride on broomsticks?
Because it's faster than walking.

What does Dracula drive?
A monster truck.

What do you call a fish's date?
His gill-friend.

What's a frog's favorite year?
A leap year.

Silly Stat: A leap year comes once every four years. Julius Caesar, a ruler of the Roman Empire, is considered the "father" of leap year because of the calendar he created based on an ancient Egyptian one. Leap day babies, born on February 29, are called "leapers" or "leaplings." A baby being born today has a 1 in 1,461 chance of being a leapling.

What do ants eat for breakfast?
Croiss-ants.

What do aliens call a zany spaceperson?
An astro-*nut*.

What type of bat loves doorbells?
A *ding*-bat.

How did the Vikings send secret messages?
Norse code.

Silly Stat: The words "Norse" and "Viking" describe the Germanic people who settled in Scandinavia during the Viking Age. They spoke a language called "Old Norse." The "Norse" refers to Norsemen (sounds like "horsemen!"), who were full-time traders.

What kind of band can't play music?
A rubber band.

What do you hold without using your hands?
Your breath.

What did the bologna say to the salami?
"Nice to meat you."

What is a snake's favorite subject in school?
Hisssssstory.

What kind of bed does a mermaid sleep in?
A waterbed.

What should you never say to a vampire when you are mad?
"Bite me!"

Why was school easier for cavemen?
Because they had no history to study.

What does a cat say when you step on its tail?
"Mee-ouch!"

What time is it when ten gorillas are chasing you?
Ten after one.

What are a plumber's favorite shoes?
Clogs.

What do ghosts say when they meet?
"How do you boo?"

Why did the computer get glasses?
To improve its website.

What dog always knows what time it is?
A watchdog.

What is a ghost's favorite tree?
Bamboo.

What do you call a boo-boo on a T. rex?
A dino-sore.

Which side of a cat has the most fur?
The outside.

Did you hear about the dog that ate a clock?
He got ticks.

What does a frog do when his car breaks down?
He gets toad away.

Why do we say "break a leg" to actors?
Because they want to be in a cast.

Silly Stat: The English expression "break a leg" is what people say to actors to wish them good luck before a performance. It is always taken as words of encouragement and has been used since Shakespeare's days. Outside of theater, it's a way to say, "Good luck! Put your best foot forward."

What day of the week are most twins born?
Twos-days.

Why did the broom get a bad grade in class?
Because it was always sweeping during class.

How do you stop a bull from charging?
You unplug it.

Why do mummies like presents?
They love the wrapping.

What's the longest word in the world?
"Smiles." There is a mile between its first and last letters.

What do you get when you cross a sponge and an electric eel?
A shock absorber.

Why did the banana go out with the blueberry?
Because she couldn't find a date.

What kind of soda does a tree like?
Root beer.

What do you call a turkey after Thanksgiving?
Lucky.

Why did the scarecrow quit his job?
Everything he did was for the birds.

What do you call a bear that loves rainy weather?
A drizzly bear.

What's a matador's favorite sandwich?
Bull-oney.

Silly Stat: Up until recently, bullfighting was a major sport in Spain. "Matador" is the name for the bullfighter, who wears a special hat as part of their costume. The two round bulbs on either side of the hat represent the bull's horns. The flattened crown of the hat is meant to look like a bull's eye.

What do you call a
walking clock?
Time travel.

What do basketball players
and babies have in common?
They're expert dribblers.

What do you get when you
cross a rabbit and a cow?
A hare in your milk.

What kind of paper
likes hip-hop?
Rapping paper.

What's a vampire's
favorite fruit?
A neck-tarine.

Why did the
computer squeak?
Someone stepped
on its mouse.

What do you call
a mean cow?
Beef jerky.

What kind of lights did
Noah use on the ark?
Floodlights.

What's the best way
to carve wood?
Whittle by whittle.

Silly Stat: Whittling is
the art of carving small
figures out of pieces
of wood. Creating tiny
works of art became a
popular pastime for men,
even General Ulysses S.
Grant, to fill their time
during the Civil War.

What time is it when you
see half a dozen chickens?
Six *o'cluck.*

What's the Joker's
favorite candy?
Snickers.

What's the noisiest sport?
Tennis—it's a racket!

What did the sun say
when it was introduced
to the earth?
"Pleased to heat you."

What do you call an eagle who plays the piano?
Talon-ted.

Silly Stat: A talon is the nail or claw of an animal and is made of a hard protein called keratin. Its many uses include digging, climbing, fighting, capturing, and holding prey. Talons are largest and most prominent on carnivorous birds, such as hawks, eagles, and owls, that need to catch and eat their prey.

What do you get when you cross a cat and a lemon?
A sourpuss.

Who makes clothes for a stegosaurus?
A dino-sewer.

What kind of horses only go out at night?
Nightmares.

Who did the mummy invite to his party?
Anybody he could dig up.

How do blue jays stay fit?
Worm-ups.

Why was the tarantula wearing a mask?
Because it was a spy-der.

What wobbles and flies?
A jelly-copter.

Why did the hamburger always lose the race?
Because it could never ketchup.

Why didn't the student get in trouble when he was caught passing notes?
Because it was music class.

What do you get when you mix history with old oil?
Ancient grease.

What sound does a metal frog make?
Rivet, rivet.

Silly Stat: Rosie the Riveter was a popular cultural icon during World War II. You might have seen her on the poster that shows her flexed arm! Her character inspired women to take jobs in factories and shipyards while men were at war. Since then, Rosie has become a symbol of equality and expanding opportunities for women in industries dominated by men.

What table doesn't have any legs?
A multiplication table.

What is always cold in the refrigerator?
Chili.

What's a teacher's favorite nation?
Explanation.

What do you call a fossil who won't go to work?
Lazy bones.

What does a vampire say to a mirror?
"Is this thing on?"

Why did the pig become an actor?
Because he was a ham.

Silly Stat: The word "ham" is used to refer to an actor who gives an exaggerated performance.

Why did the cucumber call 911?
Because he was in a pickle.

How do movie stars stay cool?
They sit next to their fans.

What do you get when you cross a bee with some meat?
A hum-burger.

Where does a television go for vacation?
Remote islands.

What did Delaware wear to the soccer game?
A New Jersey.

What do you always get for your birthday?
Older.

Why was the guy looking for fast food on his friend?
Because his friend said, "Dinner is on me."

What is a witch's favorite day of the week?
Fright-day.

Why are cats good at playing video games?
Because they have nine lives.

Silly Stat: For years, a myth developed that cats had multiple lives. In parts of Spain, it is believed that cats have seven lives, whereas Turkish and Arabic legends say cats have six lives. No one knows exactly where the expression came from, but it has been around for many years! Even William Shakespeare used the expression in his famous play *Romeo and Juliet*.

Why did Keisha put on her helmet when working on her computer?
She thought it would crash.

What do you get when you cross a refrigerator with a radio?
Cool music.

Pronounce the word M-O-S-T.
"Most."
Pronounce the word G-H-O-S-T.
"Ghost."
Pronounce the word B-O-A-S-T.
"Boast."
What do you put in the toaster?
"Toast?"
No! You put bread in the toaster and get toast out.

What asks but never answers?
An owl. ("Whooo whoooo!")

What did the werewolf eat after he got his teeth cleaned?
His dentist.

What do you call a dentist who cleans a lion's teeth?
Adventurous.

What's a pirate's favorite kind of fish?
Goldfish.

**How do you cut a
wave in half?**
With a sea-saw.

**What has 13 hearts
but no organs?**
A deck of cards.

**Why didn't the invisible
man buy a house?**
He couldn't see himself
living there.

**What do you get when
you put an iPhone
in the blender?**
Apple juice.

**What are two things you
never eat for lunch?**
Breakfast and dinner.

**What happens when an
owl gets a sore throat?**
It doesn't give a hoot.

**How many sides does
a circle have?**
Two: an inside and
an outside.

**Who is the highest-ranking
officer in a cornfield?**
The kernel.

**What did the dalmatian
say after lunch?**
"That hit the spot."

Silly Stat: Dalmatians
are often associated
with firehouses. In the
olden days, fire trucks or
carriages were pulled by
horses, but the horses
would get nervous
around fires. The
dalmatians were used
because of their ability
to keep the horses calm.

**Why are mummies
so selfish?**
Because they are all
wrapped up in themselves.

**Why did the chicken
cross the ocean?**
To get to the other tide.

**What did one snowman say
to the other snowman?**
Do you smell carrots?

Why should you put a spiderweb on your baseball glove?
To catch flies.

How do you find an archery contest?
Follow the arrows.

What do postal workers do when they get mad?
They stamp their feet.

Silly Stat: On July 1, 1847, in New York City, postage stamps first went on sale. Benjamin Franklin's face was on the five-cent stamp. George Washington was on the 10-cent stamp. It's fitting that Ben Franklin was honored, since he was the first postmaster general in the United States!

What do you call a bear without ears?
B.

What's a vampire's favorite superhero?
Batman.

What kind of nails do carpenters hate hammering?
Fingernails.

What do you call bees having a bad hair day?
Frizz-bees.

Silly Stat: Honeybees are great fliers. They fly at speeds around 15 miles per hour and beat their wings 200 times per second!

What do you call a bear with no socks on?
Bear-foot.

Why is the Hulk a good gardener?
Because he has a green thumb.

Why did the rooster cross the road?
To prove he wasn't a chicken.

What's the scariest ride at the amusement park?
The roller ghoster.

Silly Stat: The Formula Rossa in Abu Dhabi, located in the United Arab Emirates, is the fastest roller coaster in the world. It clocks in at a speed of 149.1 miles per hour! Hold on to your hat.

Why do tigers have stripes?
So they aren't spotted.

What do you call a penguin in Florida?
Lost.

How do you make a hot dog stand?
Take away its chair.

What's a woodpecker's favorite joke?
Knock, knock!

What's a duck's favorite snack?
Cheese and quackers.

Why did the witch put her broom in the washer?
She wanted a clean sweep.

Why did the octopus beat the shark in a fight?
He was well-armed.

Are monsters good at math?
Not unless you Count Dracula.

Can a kangaroo jump higher than the Statue of Liberty?
Of course! The Statue of Liberty can't jump at all.

How do you weigh a fish?
Use their scales!

Why is everyone so tired on April 1?
Because they just finished a long, 31-day March.

What do you call a flower that runs on electricity?
A power plant.

How do you stop a skunk from smelling?
Hold its nose.

> **Silly Stat:** A skunk's stripe points its way directly to the place where the smelly spray comes out! Skunks can shoot their sulfur-smelling odor up to 10 feet from their backsides. That smell can sometimes last for weeks and can be smelled as far away as a mile.

Why didn't the flower ride its bike to school?
Because the petals were broken.

What did the elephant say when it walked into the post office?
"Ouch."

Why couldn't the pirate go to the movie?
It was rated "arrrr."

How do skeletons call each other?
With tele-bones.

> **Silly Stat:** The human skeleton is made up of about 300 bones at birth. As we age, bones fuse together, bringing the total to 206 bones.

What kind of street does a ghost live on?
A dead end.

What kind of driver has no arms or legs?
A screwdriver.

What type of dogs do vampires like?
Bloodhounds.

Who delivers presents to dogs?
Santa Paws.

Why do gorillas have big nostrils?
Because they have big fingers!

What's the craziest way to travel?
Loco-motive.

Silly Stat: A locomotive is an engine that pulls a train supplying its power. Early locomotives used horses or ropes. Today, the fastest train in the world is the THSR 700T. It runs on a high-speed line between Kaohsiung and Taipei in Taiwan. It travels at 190 miles per hour! It shortens a trip of 4 hours to only 90 minutes.

What only works after it's been fired?
A rocket.

What did the dog say when he sat on sandpaper?
"Ruff."

What do you call a rabbit with fleas?
Bugs Bunny.

What animal has more lives than a cat?
A frog. It croaks every night.

Why don't ghosts like rain?
It dampens their spirits.

What do you put in a barrel to make it lighter?
A hole.

Where do you find flying rabbits?
In the hare force.

What did the porcupine say to the cactus?
"Is that you, Mom?"

Why did the baseball coach go into the kitchen?
To get a pitcher.

How much do dead batteries charge?
Nothing. They're free of charge.

Why should you be nice to the dentist?
You'll hurt his fillings.

> **Silly Stat:** Human adults usually have 32 teeth: eight incisors, four front teeth on the upper and lower jaws, four canines, eight premolars, and lastly four wisdom teeth. "Wisdom teeth" got their name because they are the last to grow, when a person is older and wiser.

What do you call an owl that does magic tricks?
Hoo-dini.

How do librarians catch fish?
With bookworms.

What do you call a belt with a watch on it?
A waist of time.

Why did the boy take a ruler to bed?
To see how long he slept.

Why was the orange so lonely?
Because the banana split.

Why was the droid angry?
Everyone kept pushing its buttons.

What are the artist's favorite shoes?
Sketchers.

How much money does a skunk have?
Too many scents.

What country do sharks come from?
Finland.

What did Neptune say to Saturn?
"Give me a ring sometime."

How do fungi clean their house?
With a mush-broom.

What do you call a sheep covered in chocolate?
A candy baaaaaa.

> **Silly Stat:** The first chocolate bar was made by Joseph Fry in England in 1847. He pressed a paste made from cocoa powder and sugar into the rectangle shape. Today, Americans eat 2.8 billion pounds, or about 11 pounds per person, of chocolate each year!

What's the quietest sport?
Bowling. You can hear a pin drop.

What did the astronaut say to the star?
"Stop spacing out."

How do you say farewell to a three-headed monster?
"Bye, bye, bye."

What happened when the cat swallowed a ball of wool?
She had mittens.

What do you call it when a cat wins at the dog show?
A cat-has-trophy.

What do you call a deer that costs a dollar?
A buck.

What did one penny say to the other penny?
We make perfect cents.

How do chickens encourage their baseball team?
They egg them on.

How much room should you give fungi to grow?
As mushroom as possible.

What time is it when a bear sits on your bed?
Time to get a new bed!

What medicine do you give a dog with a fever?
Mustard is the best thing for a hot dog.

Which side of the house do pine trees grow?
The outside.

What's a balloon's least favorite school activity?
A pop quiz.

How did Ben Franklin feel after he discovered electricity?
Shocked.

What happened when the mouse fell into the bathtub?
He came out squeaky-clean.

What's better than finding a heads-up penny?
Finding a heads-up quarter.

Silly Stat: In 2017, the United States produced over 8 billion coins to circulate in the country! Pennies, nickels, dimes, quarters, half-dollars, and dollar coins are all produced in the Philadelphia and Denver mints. These mints aren't for your breath! A mint is an industrial facility that prints money.

What's the strongest tool in the ocean?
A hammerhead shark.

Why did the little girl take a hammer to her birthday cake?
It was a pound cake.

How do hedgehogs kiss?
Very carefully.

What would a vampire never order in a restaurant?
A stake sandwich.

Silly Stat: According to vampire folklore, one of the ways to stop a vampire is to push a strong wooden or metal post called a stake through their heart.

Why don't snails fart?
Their houses don't have any windows.

Why did the doughnut visit the dentist?
It got a new filling.

How do you make an egg giggle?
You tell it a funny yolk.

What do you get when you cross a shark and a cow?
I don't know, but I wouldn't try milking it.

What do you call a messy hippo?
A hippopota-mess.

Why are giraffes slow to apologize?
It takes them a long time to swallow their pride.

What did the sink say to the dirty dishes?
"You're in hot water now."

What do you get when you cross a bunch of monkeys with an orchestra?
A chimp-phony.

What kind of hair does the ocean have?
Wavy.

What did one blade of grass say to the other during a drought?
"I guess we'll have to make dew."

Where can you find an ocean with no water?
On a map.

What does a piece of toast wear to bed?
Jammies.

Why is a sofa like a Thanksgiving turkey?
They're both filled with stuffing.

What has a bed that you can't sleep in?
A river.

Where does "Friday" come before "Monday"?
In the dictionary.

What is it called when a snowman has a temper tantrum?
A meltdown!

What did the fisherman say to the magician?
Pick a cod, any cod.

What do you call a thieving alligator?
A crook-o-dile.

Why did the cow cross the road?
To get to the udder side.

What kind of fish can perform surgery?
Sturgeons.

Silly stat: "Sturgeon" is the name for 27 species of fish that belong to the Acipenseridae family. Their evolution dates back to the Triassic period—more than 200 million years ago!

What's an astronaut's favorite part of a computer?
The space bar.

What did the red light say to the green light?
"Don't look, I'm changing."

Why did the pig get hired by the restaurant?
He was really good at bacon.

What do you call a sad puppy that likes fruit?
Melon collie.

Why do French people like to eat snails?
They can't stand fast food.

What do you get when you cross a cocker spaniel, a poodle, and a rooster?
A cocker-poodle-doo!

Why does yogurt love going to museums?
Because it's cultured.

What do you throw out when you need it and take in when you don't?
An anchor.

Why was the cat sitting on the computer?
To keep an eye on the mouse!

What's a pirate's favorite treat?
Chips ahoy, matey!

What did the baby corn ask the mommy corn?
"Where's Pop corn?"

What's a cat's favorite television show?
The evening mews.

Why don't cats play poker in the jungle?
There are too many cheetahs.

What do you call cheese that is sad?
Blue cheese.

What dog chases anything that's red?
A bulldog.

Silly Stat: Bulls (not bulldogs) have a reputation for charging when they see the color red. In fact, bulls are color-blind! It's the waving material that makes the bull charge.

What's the difference between a dog and a marine biologist?
One wags a tail and the other tags a whale.

What did the boat say to the pier?
"What's up, dock?"

Where do you find a chicken with no legs?
Anywhere you left it.

Where do cars go for a swim?
A carpool.

Why don't cats like online shopping?
They prefer a cat-alog.

What do you call blueberries playing the guitar?
A jam session.

What do you call a cat caught by the police?
A purrpetrator.

What does a grape say when it gets stepped on?
Nothing, it just lets out a little wine.

What do teddy bears do when it rains?
They get wet.

What do cats eat for breakfast?
Mice Krispies

What do dancing hens lay?
Scrambled eggs.

Why do pandas like old movies?
They prefer black-and-white film.

What do camels use to hide themselves?
Camel-flage.

Why did the cat run away from the tree?
It was scared of its bark.

What did one toilet say to the other?
You look a bit flushed.

When should you bring your dad to school?
When you have a Pop quiz.

What is the richest kind of soup?
Won-ton soup.

Silly Stat: The Korean Republic *won* is the official paper currency of South Korea. On Seollal, the Lunar New Year, South Korean children receive crisp paper money in beautiful, colorful envelopes as a gift.

Why shouldn't you tell a secret on a farm?
Because the potatoes have eyes and the corn have ears.

What's a cat's favorite dessert?
A mice-cream cone.

What are hot dogs called in winter?
Chilly dogs.

What do police officers say to their stomachs?
"You're under a vest."

What did the astronaut cook in his skillet?
Unidentified frying objects.

What do you get if you cross an apple with a shellfish?
A crab apple!

Silly Stat: There are a total of 7,500 varieties of apples grown around the world. Twenty-five hundred different types are grown in the United States. In the late 18th and early 19th centuries, John Chapman, better known as "Johnny Appleseed," planted apple orchards throughout Pennsylvania, Ohio, West Virginia, Illinois, and Indiana.

What do you get when you mix a duck with a firework?
A firequacker.

Why did the policeman give the sheep a ticket?
She made an illegal ewe turn.

How do cats get over a fight?
They hiss and make up.

How many apples grow on trees?
All of them.

2

KNOCK-KNOCK JOKES

Knock, knock.
Who's there?
Koala!
Koala who?
Koala Duty: Black Ops.

Knock, knock.
Who's there?
Fairy.
Fairy who?
**Fairy nice of you to
open the door.**

Knock, knock.
Who's there?
Peeka.
Peeka who?
Peeka-boo.

Knock, knock.
Who's there?
Jester.
Jester who?
Jester minute, I'm coming.

Silly Stat: A jester
was a person hired to
entertain kings, queens,
and their entourages.
Many of them knew how
to juggle, tell jokes, and
do magic tricks. They
wore brightly colored
clothes and funny hats.
They made up silly
songs, and sometimes
even made fun of royalty.

Knock, knock.
Who's there?
Scold.
Scold who?
**'Scold out here. I want
to come inside!**

Knock, knock.
Who's there?
Baby.
Baby who?
**Baby shark, doo, doo,
doo, doo, doo, doo.**

Knock, knock.
Who's there?
Felix.
Felix who?
Felix-hausted. Let me in.

Knock, knock.
Who's there?
Haven.
Haven who?
**Haven you heard enough of
these knock-knock jokes?**

Knock, knock.
Who's there?
Honeydew.
Honeydew who?
**Honeydew open this
door, please.**

Silly Stat: Watermelons,
cantaloupes, and
honeydew melons are
made up of 90 percent
water, making them
perfect for quenching
your thirst on a hot day!

Knock, knock.
Who's there?
Stopwatch.
Stopwatch who?
**Stopwatch you are doing
and answer the door!**

Knock, knock.
Who's there?
Mind.
Mind who?
**Mind your manners
and say "hello."**

Knock, knock.
Who's there?
Some.
Some who?
Somebody wants to visit you.

Knock, knock.
Who's there?
Doorway.
Doorway who?
**Door weigh too much,
help me open it.**

Knock, knock.
Who's there?
Iran.
Iran who?
**Iran all the way
here to tell you.**

Knock, knock.
Who's there?
Garden.
Garden who?
**Garden the door
from invaders!**

Knock, knock.
Who's there?
Needle.
Needle who?
Needle lil' help with this doorknob.

Silly Stat: Humans as far back as 12,000 years ago made needles out of animal bones, antlers, and tusks. These needles were mostly used to make fishing nets and carrying bags for the people's nomadic life. Sewing things made it possible for hunters and gatherers to carry their belongings to new territories.

Knock, knock.
Who's there?
Spin.
Spin who?
Spin a while since I've been here, let me in!

Knock, knock.
Who's there?
Heart.
Heart who?
Heart you were having a party, let me in.

Knock, knock.
Who's there?
Pizza.
Pizza who?
Pizza open the door, I'm tired of waiting.

Knock, knock.
Who's there?
Peas.
Peas who?
Peas open up, I have to go to the bathroom!

Knock, knock.
Who's there?
Oscar'd.
Oscar'd who?
Oscar'd of the dark, let me in.

Knock, knock.
Who's there?
Doe.
Doe who?
Doe, a deer, a female deer.

Silly Stat: There are 60-plus species of deer worldwide. Deer are present on all continents except Antarctica and are recognized for their beautiful antlers. Antlers are the fastest-growing living tissue in the world!

Knock, knock.
Who's there?
Nine.
Nine who?
Nine of your business.

Knock, knock.
Who's there?
Take out.
Take out who?
Take out the garbage tonight, honey!

Knock, knock.
Who's there?
Red.
Red who?
Ready or not, I'm coming in.

Knock, knock.
Who's there?
Blue.
Blue who?
Don't cry. I didn't mean to startle you.

Knock, knock.
Who's there?
Juicy.
Juicy who?
Juicy me through the window?

Knock, knock.
Who's there?
The interrupting bee.
The interrupting bee who?
"Buzzzzzz."

Knock, knock.
Who's there?
Cook.
Cook who?
Cook coo! Do you hear the clock?

Knock, knock.
Who's there?
Time.
Time who?
Time to answer the door.

Knock, knock.
Who's there?
Doctor.
Doctor Who?
I like that show, too!

Knock, knock.
Who's there?
Hawaii.
Hawaii who?
I'm fine, Hawaii you?

Knock, knock.
Who's there?
In a loop.
In a loop who?
Knock, knock.

Knock, knock.
Who's there?
House.
House who?
**House you gonna
know if you don't
answer the door?**

Knock, knock.
Who's there?
Justin.
Justin who?
**Justin time to
open the door.**

Silly Stat: *Doctor Who* is a popular science fiction television program that has been on the air for a very long time in Britain. Doctor Who is an alien who explores the universe throughout different time periods in his spaceship. To date, there have been 13 actors who have played the character Doctor Who. The newest actor is the first woman to play the role.

Knock, knock.
Who's there?
Déjà.
Déjà who?
Knock, knock.

Knock, knock.
Who's there?
Mustache.
Mustache who?
**Mustache you a question,
but I'll shave it for later!**

Silly Stat: "Déjà vu" is a French term meaning "already seen." It is described as a feeling that you've experienced something once before. On average, people who report having feelings of déjà vu say it happens to them about once per year.

Knock, knock.
Who's there?
Annabel.
Annabel who?
Annabel go ring, ring.

Knock, knock.
Who's there?
Waiter.
Waiter who?
**Waiter minute,
I'm coming in.**

Knock, knock.
Who's there?
Tex.
Tex who?
**Tex me a message
and I'll tell you.**

Knock, knock.
Who's there?
Take me.
Take me who?
Take me out to the ball game.

Knock, knock.
Who's there?
Tell.
Tell who?
Tell ya later.

Knock, knock.
Who's there?
Leaf.
Leaf who?
**Leaf what you're doing
and come here.**

**Will you remember
me in a year?**
Yes.
**Will you remember
me in a month?**
Yes.
**Will you remember
me in a second?**
Yes!
Knock, knock.
Who's there?
You forgot me already!!!

Knock, knock.
Who's there?
Weed.
Weed who?
**Weed need to open the
door to find out.**

Silly Stat: Weeds are plants that people think are bad because they grow, sometimes wildly, on their own. Of some 250,000 plant species worldwide, only about 3 percent behave like unruly weeds.

Knock, knock.
Who's there?
Toupees.
Toupees who?
Toupees in a pod.

Knock, knock.
Who's there?
Jim.
Jim who?
**Jim mind if I come in
to play with you?**

Knock, knock.
Who's there?
Fanny.
Fanny who?
**Fanny body wants to come
out, we want to play.**

Knock, knock.
Who's there?
Yo.
Yo who?
**Not yo *who*,
yo *ho*—it's a pirate!**

Knock, knock.
Who's there?
Dash.
Dash who?
**Dash a person on your
doorstep. Open the door!**

Knock, knock.
Who's there?
iPad.
iPad who?
**iPad for the pizza.
Gimme a slice!**

Knock, knock.
Who's there?
Buh.
Buh who?
Buh-bye, I'm leaving.

Knock, knock.
Who's there?
Toll.
Toll who?
**Toll you someone was
knocking at the door.**

Knock, knock.
Who's there?
Common.
Common who?
Common get it.

Knock, knock.
Who's there?
Papa Bear.
Papa Bear who?
**Papa Beary hungry
for porridge!**

Knock, knock.
Who's there?
Snow.
Snow who?
**Snow business like
show business.**

Knock, knock.
Who's there?
Broom.
Broom who?
Broom, broom, it's a motorcycle.

Knock, knock.
Who's there?
Europe.
Europe who?
Europe-ning the door?

Knock, knock.
Who's there?
Ice.
Ice who?
Ice said it was me.

Knock, knock.
Who's there?
Avenue.
Avenue who?
Avenue seen it coming?

Knock, knock.
Who's there?
Says.
Says who?
Says me, that's who.

Knock, knock.
Who's there?
Pasta.
Pasta who?
Pasta la vista, baby.

Knock, knock.
Who's there?
Omar.
Omar who?
**Omar goodness gracious,
you forgot I was visiting you.**

Knock, knock.
Who's there?
Aaron.
Aaron who?
**Aaron you gonna open
the door and find out?**

Knock, knock.
Who's there?
Shiz.
Shiz-who?
**Yes, I'm looking for
my little dog!**

Silly Stat: Shih tzus are a type of dog that originated from the country Tibet. Their name means "Little Lion." They were often given as gifts to the emperors of China.

Knock, knock.
Who's there?
Dewey.
Dewey who?
**Dewey have to keep doing
knock-knock jokes?**

Knock, knock.
Who's there?
Howl.
Howl who?
**Howl you know unless
you open the door?**

Knock, knock.
Who's there?
Heidi.
Heidi who?
**Heidi who, hidey
ho, neighbor!**

Knock, knock.
Who's there?
Police.
Police who?
Police let me in, already.

Knock, knock.
Who's there?
Yah.
Yah who?
Nah, I like Google better.

Knock, knock.
Who's there?
Hike.
Hike who?
**I didn't know you liked
Japanese poetry!**

Silly Stat: Haiku are short poems that follow a brief syllable pattern, such as 5-7-5 or 3-5-3. The poems originated in Japan. Here's an example:

Jokes slip from the tongue
To fill the heart with humor
Laughter soothes the soul

Knock, knock.
Who's there?
To.
To who?
It's "to whom."

Knock, knock.
Who's here?
Wendy.
Wendy who?
Wendy bell gonna get fixed?

Knock, knock.
Who's there?
Iva.
Iva who?
Iva sore hand from all this knocking.

Knock, knock.
Who's there?
Otto.
Otto who?
Otto know either, do you?

Knock, knock.
Who's there?
Shamp.
Shamp who?
Thanks, my hair was kind of dirty!

Knock, knock.
Who's there?
Roach.
Roach who?
Roach you a text, didn't you read it?

Knock-knock.
Who's there?
Tune-y.
Tune-y who?
Tune-y fish.

Knock, knock.
Who's there?
Iron.
Iron who?
Iron the right to run free!

Knock, knock.
Who's there?
Chick.
Chick who?
Chick the peephole and you'll find out.

Knock, knock.
Who's there?
'Sup.
'Sup who?
'Sup, buttercup?

Knock, knock.
Who's there?
Amanda.
Amanda who?
Amanda fix your doorbell.

Knock, knock.
Who's there?
Nicholas.
Nicholas who?
A Nicholas not much money these days.

Knock, knock.
Who's there?
Candice.
Candice who?
Candice be the last knock-knock joke?

Knock, knock.
Who's there.
Jada.
Jada who?
Jada say the word and I'll stop.

Knock, knock.
Who's there?
Nuisance.
Nuisance who?
What's nuisance yesterday?

Knock, knock.
Who's there?
Dolphin.
Dolphin who?
Dolphin make no difference, open the door.

Silly Stat: Dolphins live in groups that hunt and play together. Large groups of dolphins are called "pods" and can have 1,000 members or more. Dolphins are carnivores. Fish, squid, and crustaceans are included in their diet. A 260-pound dolphin eats about 33 pounds of fish a day.

Knock, knock.
Who's there?
Asparagus.
Asparagus who?
Asparagus doesn't have a last name.

Knock, knock.
Who's there?
Goliath.
Goliath who?
**Goliath down, thou
look-eth tired!**

Knock, knock.
Who's there?
An extraterrestrial.
An extraterrestrial who?
**Wait, how many
extraterrestrials
do you know?!**

Knock, knock.
Who's there?
Control Freak.
Con—
**Okay, now you say,
"Control Freak who?!"**

Knock, knock.
Who's there?
Snow.
Snow who?
**Snow use. I forgot
my name again!**

Knock, knock.
Who's there?
Closure.
Closure who?
**Closure book and
open the door!**

Knock, knock.
Who's there?
Ho-ho.
Ho-ho who?
**You know, your Santa
impression could
use a little work.**

Knock, knock.
Who's there?
Aiden Snufflemount.
Aiden Snufflemount who?
**Oh, come on, how many
"Aiden Snufflemounts"
do you know?**

Knock, knock.
Who's there?
Rhino.
Rhino who?
**Rhino every knock-knock
joke there is!**

Knock, knock.
Who's there?
Witches.
Witches who?
**Witches the way
to the movies?**

Knock, knock.
Who's there?
Ice-Cream Soda.
Ice-Cream Soda who?
**Ice-Cream Soda whole
neighborhood can hear!**

Knock, knock.
Who's there?
Zany.
Zany who?
Zanybody home?

Knock, knock.
Who's there?
Jess.
Jess who?
Jess open the door.

Knock, knock.
Who's there?
Noise.
Noise who?
Noise to see you!

Knock, knock.
Who's there?
Conrad.
Conrad who?
**Conrad-ulations! That was
a good knock-knock joke.**

Knock, knock.
Who's there?
Razor.
Razor who?
**Razor hands and dance
through the doorway!**

Knock, knock.
Who's there?
Bruce.
Bruce who?
**I Bruce easily, my fingers
are stuck in the door!**

Knock, knock.
Who's there?
Ears.
Ears who?
**Ears another knock-knock
joke for you!**

Knock, knock.
Who's there?
Ferdie!
Ferdie who?
**Ferdie last time—
open this door!**

Knock, knock.
Who's there?
Keanu.
Keanu who?
**Keanu let me in,
it's cold out here.**

Knock, knock.
Who's there?
Claire.
Claire who?
**Claire the doorway,
I'm coming in!**

Knock, knock.
Who's there?
Nobel.
Nobel who?
Nobel, so I guess I'll knock.

Knock, knock.
Who's there?
Value.
Value who?
Value be my Valentine?

Knock, knock.
Who's there.
Amish.
Amish who?
Amish you so much!

Knock, knock.
Who's there?
Howie.
Howie who?
**Howie gonna get
in the house?**

Knock, knock.
Who's there?
Theodore.
Theodore who?
Theodore between us.

Knock, knock.
Who's there?
Grandma.
Grandma who?
Knock, knock.
Who's there?
Grandma.
Grandma who?
Knock, knock.
Who's there?
Aunt.
Aunt who?
**Aunt you glad I didn't
say "Grandma"?**

Knock, knock.
Who's there?
Toby.
Toby who?
**Toby or not to be?
That is the question.**

Knock, knock.
Who's there?
Wire.
Wire who?
Wire you asking me that?

Knock, knock.
Who's there?
Owl.
Owl who?
Owl aboard!

Knock, knock.
Who's there?
Weirdo.
Weirdo who?
**Weirdo you think
you're going?**

Knock, knock.
Who's there?
Cozy.
Cozy who?
**Cozy who's knocking
at the door.**

Knock, knock.
Who's there?
R2.
R2 who?
R2-D2.

Knock, knock.
Who's there?
Wood ant.
Wood ant who?
**Wood ant be knocking if I
didn't need to come inside.**

Knock, knock.
Who's there?
Baby owl.
Baby Owl who?
**Baby Owl use the back
door next time.**

Knock, knock.
Who's there?
Safari.
Safari who?
Sa-fari, so good.

Knock, knock.
Who's there?
2:30.
2:30 who?
**I made an appointment
with the dentist because
my 2:30 (tooth-hurty).**

Knock, knock.
Who's there?
Gopher.
Gopher who?
**Gopher some ice
cream together?**

Knock, knock.
Who's there?
Herring.
Herring who?
**Herring some terrible
knock-knock jokes!**

Knock, knock.
Who's there?
Who.
Who who?
Sorry, I don't speak owl!

Knock, knock.
Who's there?
Nota.
Nota who?
**Nota 'nother
knock-knock joke.**

Knock, knock.
Who's there?
Rita.
Rita who?
**Rita note and then
you'll know.**

Knock, knock.
Who's there?
Pasture.
Pasture who?
**Pasture bedtime, but
I'm knocking anyway.**

Knock, knock.
Who's there?
Waiter.
Waiter who?
**Waiter minute, I have
to put on my jacket.**

Knock, knock.
Who's there?
Geese.
Geese who?
I'm not telling you!

Knock, knock.
Who's there?
Tish.
Tish who?
**Tish-who for your
runny nose?**

Knock, knock.
Who's there?
Radio.
Radio who?
Radio not, here I come.

Knock, knock.
Who's there?
Kenya.
Kenya who?
Kenya feel the love tonight?

Knock, knock.
Who's there?
Yetta.
Yetta who?
**Yetta 'nother
knock-knock joke.**

Knock, knock.
Who's there?
Armenia.
Armenia who?
Armenia every word I say!

Knock, knock.
Who's there?
Butcher.
Butcher who?
**Butcher left leg in,
butcher left leg out!**

Knock, knock.
Who's there?
Surgeon.
Surgeon who?
Surgeon thou shalt find.

Silly Stat: Old English is one of the first forms of the English language. It was used from 450 CE to 1100 CE throughout England. It sounds a little bit like German. It is very different from the English we speak today!

Knock, knock.
Who's there?
Heart.
Heart who?
**Heart you the first
time, don't yell!**

Knock, knock.
Who's there?
Wood.
Wood who?
**Wood you do me a favor
and open the door?**

Knock, knock.
Who's there?
**R-U-N. (Hint: read the
letters, not the whole word.)**
R-U-N who?
R-U-N the car yet?

Knock, knock.
Who's there?
Ooze!
Ooze who?
Ooze in charge around here?

Knock, knock.
Who's there?
Letter.
Letter who?
**Letter in or she'll knock
down the door!**

Knock, knock.
Who's there?
Sweden.
Sweden who?
Sweden sour chicken!

Knock, knock.
Who's there?
Icing.
Icing who?
**Icing so loudly that
everyone can hear me!**

Knock, knock.
Who's there?
Godiva.
Godiva who?
**Godiva terrible headache,
do you have an aspirin?**

Knock, knock.
Who's there?
Handsome.
Handsome who?
**Handsome sunscreen
over, the sun is blazing!**

Knock, knock.
Who's there?
Nuff.
Nuff who?
**Nuff knock-knock
jokes, please.**

Knock, knock.
Who's there?
Dishes.
Dishes who?
**Dishes the last
knock-knock joke.**

3

TONGUE TWISTERS

**Many mumbling mice are making
merry music in the moonlight.**

Truly rural.

Specific Pacific.

Selfish shellfish.

Silly Stat: Lobsters taste with their legs and chew with their stomachs. Their nervous system is similar to those of grasshoppers and ants. Sometimes they are called "bugs."

Silly sushi chef.

Six silly socks.

Daddy draws doors.

Shine so shiny.

Ed had edited it.

She saw Sam.

She shifts sheep.

Willie's really weary.

Wren rents right.

She steals cheese.

Bake big batches.

Fresh fried fish.

World Wide Web.

Blue box hot ox.

Two twirled 'til ten.

Octopus ocular optics.

Friendly fleas and fireflies.

Cooks cook cupcakes quickly.

Zebras zig and zebras zag.

The blue bluebird blinks.

Raw wretched rain runs.

Still sell silk shirts.

Fred fed four frogs.

Ralph rode red roadsters.

Wanda watches whales
on Wednesdays.

Six slimy snails
sailed silently.

Buck bought burros best.

Quick kiss, quick
kiss, quick kiss.

Silly Stat: "*Burro*" is the Spanish word for "donkey." Donkeys have incredibly strong memories. They can recognize areas they haven't seen for up to 25 years!

Pad kid poured curd
pulled cod.

She threw three free throws.

Shave a single shingle thin.

Fetch four fine fresh fish.

Susie sits silver seats.

Green glass globes
gently glowing.

Rubber baby buggy bumpers.

A snake sneaks to seek a snack.

Nine nimble newts
nibbling nuts.

Not these things here,
but those things there.

She should shun
the shining sun.

Tim threw three
thumbtacks.

Silly Stat: The world's oldest chewing gum is 9,000 years old. Many old civilizations enjoyed the pastime of chewing gum. The ancient Greeks chewed *mastic*, whereas the ancient Mayan Indians were busy chomping on *chicle*.

She fed six sheep cheap chow.

Twelve twins
twirled 12 twigs.

Thinkers thinking thick
thoughtful thoughts.

We shall surely see
the sunshine soon.

I like New York, unique New York, I like unique New York.

Two tiny timid toads trying
to trot to Tarrytown.

Lucky rabbits revel
in ruckus.

Silly Stat: The big difference between frogs and toads is that frogs need to live near water to survive, whereas toads do not. Toads have drier, wart-covered, leathery skin and shorter legs than frogs. That's why some species of toads can be found in deserts, where water is hard to find.

Silly Stat: A female rabbit is called a "doe." A male rabbit is called a "buck." A young rabbit is called a "kit." More than half of the world's rabbits live in North America.

I looked right at Larry's
rally and left in a hurry.

I wish to wash my
wristwatch.

Three gray geese in
green fields grazing.

Wrecked sets right
where you went.

Two towels tossed
toward toes.

Four furious friends
fought for the phone.

A really leery Larry rolls
readily to the road.

I saw a sight; the
sight saw me.

Rory's lawn rake rarely
rakes really right.

Night nurses nursing
nicely nightly.

Watch right, right watch.

The big bug bit the
little beetle.

Silly Stat: Beetles live everywhere. Did you know that one out of every four animals on Earth is a beetle? Most adult beetles wear shells like body armor and can vary in size. The largest beetle, a *Titanus giganteus*, can grow up to six and a half inches in size!

The cat catchers can't
catch caught cats.

Little Lillian lets lazy lizards
lie along the lily pads.

Fred fed Ted bread, and
Ted fed Fred bread.

A bragging baker
baked black bread.

Silly Stat: In London, fire broke out at Thomas Farriner's bakery on Pudding Lane a little after midnight on Sunday, September 2, 1666. The fire destroyed some 13,200 homes, plus 84 churches and other important buildings such as the Royal Exchange, Guildhall, and St. Paul's Cathedral. More than 100,000 people were left homeless. But one good thing came out of the fire: It destroyed most of the rats infecting people with the plague, stopping the deadly disease!

Send toast to ten tense temps in ten tall tents.

Three fluffy feathers fell from Phyllis's flimsy fan.

Each Easter Eddie eats 80 Easter eggs.

I saw Sherry sitting in a shoeshine shop.

On a lazy laser raiser lies a laser ray eraser.

Silly Stat: The word "laser" is actually an acronym for "light amplification by stimulated emission of radiation." The strength of early lasers was measured in Gillettes (yes, like the razor!). In 1960, Theodore Maiman measured the strength of a laser by the number of razor blades a beam could cut through.

If cows could fly, I'd have a cow pie in my eye.

Lions loan lots of lottery letters lately.

"Surely Sylvia swims!" shrieked Sammy, surprised.

The boot band brought the black boot back.

Vincent vowed vengeance very vehemently.

Letty lets lovely levers level lazily.

A skunk sat on a stump and thunk the stump
stunk, but the stump thunk the skunk stunk.

How much pot could a
pot roast roast, if a pot
roast could roast pot?

Betty and Bob brought
back blue balloons
from the big bazaar.

Silly stat: Balloons
galore! Did you know
that before toy balloons
were invented, people
made balloons by
inflating pig bladders
and animal intestines?
Later came the hot-air
balloon created by the
Montgolfier brothers,
which was designed
to help people travel
by flight. The brothers
launched a giant balloon
with a passenger basket
on November 21, 1783.

How many yaks could
a yak pack pack if a yak
pack could pack yaks?

Six sheep sleep on silk sheets.

Pat the fat black cat
on the back.

If there never was an ever,
then the ever was not never.

How can a clam cram in
a clean cream can?

Ryan ran rings around
the Roman ruins.

If Stu chews shoes,
should Stu choose the
shoes he chews?

Six sick chicks nick six slick
bricks with picks and sticks.

Don't be late at the gate for
our date at a quarter to eight.

Lesser leather never
weathered wetter
weather better.

I saw a saw that could
out-saw any other
saw I ever saw.

Does your sport shop stock
short socks with spots?

Rory the warrior and Roger the worrier read rapidly in rural Raleigh.

A tricky, frisky shrimp with sixty super scaly stripes sips soapy soda in the slick sunshine.

Any noise annoys an oyster, but a noisy noise annoys an oyster more.

Silly Stat: Oysters grow on reefs that provide a natural barrier to storm waves and rising sea levels. They absorb as much as 76 to 93 percent of wave energy, which reduces erosion, flooding, and property damage when there are coastal storms like hurricanes. Oyster reefs are in great danger from overfishing and pollution.

A big bug bit the little beetle but the little beetle bit the big bug back.

If you notice this notice, you will notice that this notice is not worth notice.

I am not a pheasant-plucker, but a pheasant-plucker's son. And I am only plucking pheasants 'til the pheasant-plucker comes.

If two witches were watching two watches, which witch would watch which watch?

Swan swam over the sea—swim, swan, swim! Swan swam back again—well swum, swan!

If you must cross a coarse, cross cow across a crowded cow-crossing, cross the cross, coarse cow across the crowded cow-crossing carefully.

4

Puns & One-Liners

What's Moby Dick's favorite dinner?
Fish and *ships.*

Currently, the flower business is *blooming*.

You have cat to be *kitten me right meow*.

The best way to communicate with fish is to *drop them a line*.

Let *minnow* what you think.

> **Silly Stat:** The term "minnow" describes any small, silvery fish. Most species of minnows are less than four inches in length and have a relatively short life span of three to four years. Larger minnow varieties can live for up to 10 years.

What is every whale's favorite greeting? *Whale* hello there!

What did the lawyer name his daughter? *Sue.*

What did the hamburger name its baby? *Patty!*

When is a tire a bad singer? When it's *flat*.

Why do bees hum? They don't know *the words*.

Never tell a bald guy a *hair-raising* story.

I wrote a song about a tortilla. Well actually, it's more of a *wrap*.

Why are eggs not into jokes? Because they could *crack up*.

What's a chicken's favorite vegetable? *Eggplant.*

This gravity joke is getting a bit old, but I *fall for it* every time.

Want to go on a picnic?
Alpaca lunch.

Silly Stat: Alpacas were domesticated by the Incas in South America more than 6,000 years ago and raised for their beautiful wool. Alpaca fiber is much like sheep's wool, but warmer and not itchy. Most people find they are not allergic to it. Because of their calm and gentle nature, alpacas are used in some countries as therapy animals.

If you need help building
an ark, I *Noah* guy.

How do trees get online?
They just *log in.*

Why was the chef arrested?
She was *beating the eggs.*

Pencils could be made with
erasers at both ends, but
what would be *the point*?

He wears glasses during math
because it improves *division.*

I wasn't originally going to
get a brain transplant, but
then I *changed my mind.*

Don't spell "part"
backward. It's a *trap.*

I'm reading a book
about gravity.
It's impossible to *put down.*

Don't trust atoms, they
make up everything.

What do you call the
security outside of a
Samsung store?
Guardians of the Galaxy.

I accidentally handed
my brother a glue stick
instead of a ChapStick.
He still isn't talking to me.

When I lose the TV
controller, it's always hidden
in some *remote* location.

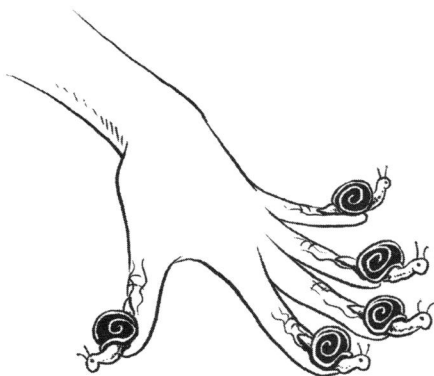

Where do you find
giant snails?
On the ends of giants' fingers.

Did you hear about the
kidnapping at school?
It's okay, he woke up.

RIP, boiled water.
You will be mist.

My teacher told me to "have
a good day," so I *went home.*

Why do dragons sleep all day?
They like to hunt **knights**.

Silly Stat: Dragons are mythical creatures written about in the folklore of many cultures since the beginning of civilization. Dragons generally have reptilian characteristics and can be helpful and guardian-like, although others are vicious and deadly. When the first dinosaur bones were discovered years ago, people thought the large bones were those of dragons.

Did you hear about the new auto body shop? It comes highly *wreck-a-mended*.

What sound does a sleeping T. rex make? A *dino-snore*.

I'm glad I know sign language, it's pretty *handy*.

Silly Stat: Sign language varies around the world. Even in the same country, sign language can have different dialects or ways of speaking. In North America, people use American Sign Language.

How much money does a pirate pay for corn? A *buccaneer*.

Don't interrupt your mother when she is working on a puzzle. You'll hear some *crosswords*.

Did you hear that the coin factory closed down yesterday? It doesn't make any *cents*.

Have you ever heard of an honest *cheetah*?

Silly stat: When cheetahs are running at full speed, their stride (length between steps) is six to seven meters, or about 21 feet. Their feet only the touch ground twice during each stride.

Knowing how to pick locks has really *opened a lot of doors* for me.

A friend wanted to have a contest with bird puns, but *toucan* play that game.

If a wild pig kills you, does it mean you've been *boared* to death?

How did the turkey win the talent show?
With its *drumsticks.*

Vegans believe meat eaters and butchers are gross. But those who sell you fruit and vegetables are **grocer.**

Jokes about unemployed people are not funny. They just **don't work.**

Did you hear police arrested the World Tongue Twister Champion? I imagine he'll be given a **tough sentence.**

Why is Peter Pan always flying? He **neverlands.**

What did the librarian say when the books were in a mess? We ought to be ashamed of **our shelves!**

What do baseball players eat on? Home plates!

What do you call a musician with problems? A **trebled** man.

What's an avocado's favorite music? **Guac** 'n' roll.

Silly Stat: Did you know that avocados are a fruit and not a vegetable? Avocados are an Aztec symbol of love and fertility because they grow in pairs on trees. Avocados are not only the main ingredient in guacamole and an addition to sandwiches and salads; in some places, such as Brazil, people also add avocados to ice cream!

What do you call a musical cow? A **moo**-sician.

I've started sleeping in our fireplace. Now I sleep like a **log!**

What's a golf club's favorite type of music? Swing.

Someone sent 10 different puns to friends, with the hope that at least one of the puns would make them laugh. No pun *in 10* did.

I'm going to buy some Velcro for my shoes instead of laces. Why *knot*?

Did you hear about the new gym that shut down? It just didn't *work out*.

Why did the pianist keep banging his head against the keys? He was playing *by ear*.

Did you hear about the boy who tried to catch fog? He *mist*.

I went to a seafood disco last week and pulled a *mussel*.

Long fairy tales have a tendency to *dragon*.

Why was the teacher cross-eyed? Her *pupils* got out of control.

Peacocks are meticulous because they show attention to *de tail*.

Silly Stat: Technically, only male peafowl are called "peacocks." Female peafowl are referred to as "peahens." Babies are called "peachicks." Male peachicks don't start growing their showy trains until about age three, but a full-grown peacock's tail feathers can reach up to six feet long and make up about 60 percent of its body's length. Despite their large size, peacocks do fly.

What did the dolphin say after he accidentally swam into another sea creature? I didn't do it on porpoise.

What is Beethoven doing now?
De-composing.

Silly Stat: German composer Ludwig van Beethoven is known for creating nine symphonies, five concertos for the piano, 32 piano sonatas, and 16 string quartets. He also composed other chamber music, choral works, and songs, all while losing his hearing. By the time he was 31, Beethoven had lost 60 percent of his hearing. Eventually, he went totally deaf.

Somebody stole all my lamps.
I couldn't be more *de-lighted!*

Who is the penguin's favorite aunt?
Aunt-Arctica!

Did you hear about the skunk that fell in the river?
It *stank* to the bottom.

Why did the chicken cross the playground?
To get to the other *slide.*

Isn't it scary that doctors call what they do "*practice*"?

Hung a picture up on the wall the other day.
Nailed it.

Did you hear about the two antennas who met on a roof, fell in love, and got married?
The ceremony wasn't much, but the reception was excellent.

What is brown, hairy, and wears sunglasses?
A coconut on vacation.

The cats not feline well?
Call a *purrimedic.*

How do construction workers party?
They raise the *roof.*

I told my mom that I was going
to make a bike out of spaghetti.
You should have seen her face
when I rode **straight pasta.**

How does a gorilla
ring the doorbell?
King Kong! King Kong!

Did you hear about the
angry bird that landed
on a doorknob?
It really flew *off the handle*.

What days do mothers
have baby boys?
Son-days.

I broke my finger yesterday.
On the other hand, I'm okay.

What did the buffalo
say when his son went
off to college?
"Bison."

If you spent your day in
a well, can you say your
day was *well-spent*?

What sort of TV shows
do ducks watch?
*Duck*umentaries.

What did the dad spider
say to the baby spider?
You spend too much
time on the *web*.

If you're scared of
elevators, start taking
steps to avoid them.

Some people say I'm
addicted to somersaults,
but that's just *how I roll*.

I was hoping to steal some
leftovers from the party, but
I guess my plans were *foiled*.

Silly Stat: The United States first produced aluminum foil in 1913 to use in making identification leg bands for racing pigeons! That same year, Life Savers was founded and began wrapping its Pep O Mint candies in tinfoil to keep them fresh.

What's the worst part about movie theater candy prices? They're always *Raisinet*.

I went to buy some camouflage pants the other day, but I *couldn't find any*.

> **Silly Stat:** The first official permanent movie theater was located on Main Street in Buffalo, New York. It was opened on Monday, October 19, 1896, by Thomas Edison. It seated more than 70 people. At the time, the theater showed mostly travel films, but people were amazed to see moving pictures on a large screen!

My roommates are concerned that I'm using their kitchen utensils, but that's a *whisk* I'm willing to take.

Did you hear about the woman who sued the airport for misplacing her luggage? She *lost* her case.

How can you tell if a vampire has a cold? He starts *coffin*.

My uncle bought a donkey because he thought he might get a *kick out of it*.

Did you hear about the guy who was admitted to the hospital with a horse in his stomach? Don't worry, his condition is *stable*.

In the winter my dog wears his coat, but in the summer, he wears his coat and *pants*.

When a new hive is done, bees have a house-*swarming* party.

Thanks for explaining the word "many" to me; *it means a lot*.

5

RIDDLES

Riddles can be hoot-hollerin' funny. And sometimes, they're so tricky they're a joke! Can you scratch your noggin and solve the following riddles?

(Answers are on 258.)

1. What is as big as an elephant,
but weighs nothing at all?

2. The more you take away, the larger it becomes. What is it?

3. What has many rings, but no fingers?

4. What five-letter word becomes shorter when you add two letters to it?

5. Why would a man living in New York not be buried in Chicago?

6. What can honk without a horn?

7. What has a horn but doesn't honk?

> **Silly Stat:** The Willis Tower (formerly known as "Sears Tower") is one of Chicago's most popular tourist attractions. It is the third-tallest building in the Western Hemisphere. On a clear day, visitors can see four states from the Skydeck: Illinois, Indiana, Wisconsin, and Michigan.

8. What's a 10-letter word that starts with gas?

9. You can you serve it, but never eat it. What is it?

10. What kind of coat can you only put on when it is wet?

11. What flies around all day but never goes anywhere?

12. What ship has two mates, but no captain?

13. Which candles burn longer, tallow or beeswax?

14. What is only a small box but can weigh over a hundred pounds?

15. What travels around the world but stays in one spot?

16. Why would a baby ant be confused when he looks at his family?

17. What always sleeps with its shoes on?

18. I am a word. If you pronounce me right, it will be wrong. If you pronounce me wrong, it will be right. What word am I?

19. A farmer has 10 chickens, five horses, two children, and a wife. How many feet are on the farm?

20. A taxi driver is going the wrong way down a one-way street. He passes four police officers, but none of them stop him. Why?

21. Mr. Blue lives in the Blue House. Mrs. Yellow lives in the Yellow House. Mr. Orange lives in the Orange House. Who lives in the White House?

Silly Stat: At various times throughout history, the White House has been known as the "President's Palace," the "President's House," and the "Executive Mansion." President Theodore Roosevelt officially gave the White House its current name in 1901. In the White House, there are 412 doors, 147 windows, 28 fireplaces, eight staircases, and three elevators.

22. You can hear it, but you can't touch or see it. It is unique to you, but everyone has one. What is it?

23. They come out at night without being called. They are lost during the day without being stolen. What are they?

24. There were five people under an umbrella. Why didn't they get wet?

Silly Stat: The word "umbrella" comes from the Latin word "*umbros*," which means "shade" or "shadow." The first use of umbrellas was as a parasol, to protect people from the sun.

25. Why would a boy bury his flashlight?

Silly Stat: A 2,200-year-old clay jar found near Baghdad, Iraq, has been loosely described as the oldest-known electric battery in existence. This ancient technology was discovered at a Mesopotamian archaeological dig.

26. I appear where there is light, but if a light shines on me, I disappear. What am I?

27. What seven letters did Sophie say when she saw the refrigerator had no food?

28. What happens once in a lifetime, twice in a moment, but never in one hundred years?

29. If April showers bring May flowers, what do Mayflowers bring?

30. I can be shaped, but never come free. I drive people crazy for the love of me. What am I?

31. What do you call a man who does not have all his fingers on one hand?

32. A woman is 20 years old, but only had five birthdays in her life. How?

33. What is put on a table and cut, but is never eaten?

Silly Stat: There are 52 cards in a standard deck. There are 52 weeks in a year, and if you add up all the symbols in a deck of cards, plus a "1" for each joker, the sum equals the number of days in a leap year: 366.

34. I have no life, but I can die; what am I?

35. You walk into a room with a match, a kerosene lamp, a candle, and a fireplace. What do you light first?

36. I'm always on the table for dinner, but you don't get to eat me. What am I?

37. What do you find in water that never gets wet?

38. What is easy to lift, but hard to throw?

39. What has two heads, four eyes, six legs, and a tail?

40. Why is the Mississippi such an unusual river?

41. What can go up the chimney when down, but cannot go down the chimney when up?

42. What word contains 26 letters, but only has three syllables?

43. What has a bottom at the top of it?

44. Forward I am heavy, but backward I am not. What am I?

45. What is at the end of everything?

46. The more you take, the more you leave behind. What are they?

47. A lawyer, a plumber, and a hatmaker walk down the street. Who has the biggest hat?

48. Three doctors said that Bill is their brother. Bill says he has no brothers. How many brothers does Bill actually have?

49. A little girl goes to the store and buys one dozen eggs. As she goes home, all but three break. How many eggs are left unbroken?

50. A girl fell off a 20-foot ladder. She wasn't hurt. Why?

51. I go around all of the cities, towns, and villages, but never come inside. What am I?

52. A man leaves home and turns left three times, only to return home facing two men wearing masks. Who are those two men?

53. What English word begins and ends with the same three letters?

54. People make me, save me, change me, and raise me. What am I?

55. What three letters turn a child into an adult?

56. What is higher without a head than it is with it?

57. What comes down, but never goes up?

Bonus Math Riddle!
Can you write down eight eights so that they add up to one thousand?

58. You find me in December, but not any other month. What am I?

59. What bet can never be won?

60. A word in this sentence is misspelled. What word is it?

61. I can be broken, but I never move. I can be closed and opened. I am sealed by hands. What am I?

62. I am often following you and copying your every move. Yet you can never touch me or catch me. What am I?

63. A man describes his daughters by saying, "They are all blonde but two, all brunette but two, and all redheaded but two." How many daughters does he have?

64. What type of dress can never be worn?

65. What four-letter word can be written forward, backward, or upside down, and can still be read from left to right?

66. I have hundreds of limbs but cannot walk. What am I?

67. I don't have eyes, ears, a nose, or a tongue, but I can see, smell, hear, and taste everything. What am I?

68. What cannot speak or hear anything, but always tells the truth?

Silly Stat: Some mirrors can reflect sound waves as well as reflect images. These mirrors are known as acoustic mirrors. Before the development of radar, mirrors were used in World War II to detect sounds coming from enemy aircraft.

69. What fruit can you use to sip water?

70. What has bark, but no bite?

71. I am a word of letters three; add two and fewer there will be. What word am I?

72. What can clap without any hands?

73. What word is pronounced the same if you take away four of its five letters?

74. If you drop me I'm sure to crack, but give me a smile and I'll always smile back. What am I?

75. What is black when you buy it, red when you use it, and gray when you throw it away?

76. I turn once; what is out will not get in. I turn again; what is in will not get out. What am I?

77. How does the kid cross the river without getting wet?

78. What is in the middle of the sky?

79. You can break me without touching or seeing me. What am I?

80. What wears a jacket, but no pants?

Silly Stat: Bill Gates bought the Codex Leicester, a collection of scientific writings by artist and scientist Leonardo da Vinci, for more than $30 million!

81. Take away my first letter, and I still sound the same. Take away my last letter, I still sound the same. Even take away my letter in the middle, I will still sound the same. I am a five-letter word. What am I?

82. It has eyes that cannot see, a tongue that cannot taste, and a soul that cannot die. What is it?

83. What has its heart in its head?

84. You can keep it only after giving it away to someone. What is it?

85. It has been around for millions of years but is no more than a month old. What is it?

86. What hangs all day and burns all night?

87. What loses its head in the morning, but gets it back at night?

Silly Stat: Scientists say the moon was made when a rock smashed into Earth. The most widely accepted explanation is that the moon was created when a rock the size of Mars slammed into Earth, shortly after the solar system began forming about 4.5 billion years ago. Currently, the moon is drifting away from Earth. It is moving approximately 3.8 centimeters away from our planet every year.

88. What is round on both sides but high in the middle?

89. What can point in every direction, but can't reach the destination by itself?

90. What type of cheese is made backward?

> **Silly Stat:** Edam is a slightly hard cheese that first came from the Netherlands. It is named after a town called Edam, located in North Holland. Look for its waxy red rind in the grocery store.

91. How do you spell "mousetrap"?

92. What runs all day but never gets anywhere?

93. What goes up and down, but never moves?

94. What goes in and around the house but never touches it?

95. What match can't you put in a matchbox?

96. I babble but I can't talk. What am I?

97. I make two people out of one. What am I?

98. Take one out and scratch my head; I am now black but was once yellow and red. What am I?

99. Where do four queens stay when they are not in a castle?

100. With pointed fangs, I sit and wait. With piercing force, I snap my bait. What am I?

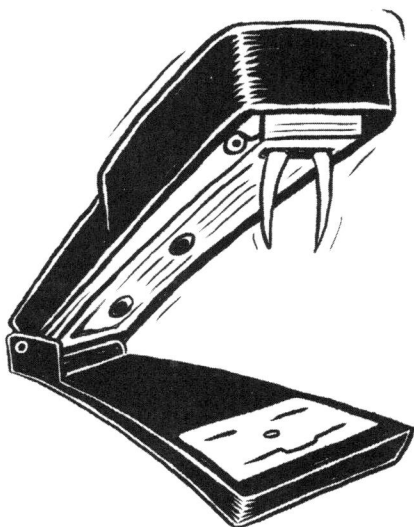

Silly Stat: The first known stapler was made in the 18th century in France for King Louis XV. Legend has it that the staples were made from gold, encrusted with precious stones, and bore his Royal Court's insignia. The growing use of paper in the 19th century created a demand for an efficient paper fastener. Modern staplers can be traced to a patent filed by Henry R. Heyl in Philadelphia, in 1877.

101. What part of London is in Brazil?

102. What has a neck and no head, two arms and no hands?

103. As I went across the bridge, I met a man with a load of wood, which was neither straight nor crooked. What kind of wood was it?

104. I am the mightiest weapon, but I've never fired a shot. What am I?

105. What breaks yet never falls, and what falls yet never breaks?

106. I saw an unusual book. The foreword comes after the epilogue. The end is in the first half of the book. The index comes before the introduction. Name that book.

107. I am so simple, I can only point. Yet I guide men all over the world. What am I?

108. What man cannot live in a house?

109. We are twins. We are close together, but we don't touch. We are far apart, yet we become one. What are we?

110. A house of wood in a hidden place, built without nails or glue. High above the ground, I hold something precious. What am I?

111. I can sizzle like bacon, but am made with an egg. I have plenty of backbone but lack a leg. I peel layers like an onion, but still remain whole. I'm long like a flagpole yet fit in a hole. What am I?

Bonus Math Riddle!
If 11 plus two equals 1, 9 plus five equals what?

112. I'm never thirsty, but I always drink. What am I?

113. A frog jumped into a pot of cream and started treading. It soon felt something solid under its feet. How was the frog able to hop out?

114. A horse is on a 24-foot chain and wants an apple that is 26 feet away. How did the horse reach the apple?

115. Dead on the field lie 10 soldiers in white, knocked down by three eyes, dark as night. What happened?

Silly Stat: Bowling is a very old game and dates as far back as 3200 BCE in Ancient Egypt. Modern bowling is a few thousand years younger: Indoor bowling lanes opened up in 1840 in New York City, but only men bowled at the time. Women were not allowed to bowl until 1917!

116. Turn me on my spine, open me up, and you'll be the wisest of all time. Who am I?

117. I have both face and tail, but I am not alive. Who am I?

118. I can seize and hold the wind. My touch brings giggles. Who am I?

119. The wise humans are sure of it. Even the fools know it. The rich want it. The greatest of heroes fear it. Yet the lowliest of cowards would die for it. What is it?

120. Through wind and rain, I love to play. I roam the earth, yet here I stay. I can crumble stones, and fire cannot burn me. Yet I am soft, and you can dent me with your hand. Who am I?

121. Flesh as red as blood with a heart of stone. What am I?

122. A girl is sitting in a house at night that has no lights on at all. There is no lamp, no candle, nothing to brighten the room. Yet, she is reading. How?

123. It lives in winter, dies in summer, and grows down with its roots on top. What is it?

124. How can somebody walk for eight days without sleeping?

125. You had 20 people build your house in two months. How long would it take 10 people to build the very same house?

126. I have 100 legs but cannot stand. A long neck but no head. What am I?

127. Remove the outside, cook the inside, eat the outside, throw away the inside. What am I?

128. What common English verb becomes its own past tense by rearranging its letters?

129. If you have a cube, each edge two inches long, how many total square inches are there on all eight sides?

130. Is it correct to say, "the yolk of eggs is white" or "the yolk of eggs are white"?

131. Is it legal for a man to marry his widow's sister?

132. I have no sword, I have no spear, yet rule a horde that many fear. My soldiers fight with wicked sting, I rule with might, yet am no king. What am I?

133. My forks are here; my forks are there. They're not on the table, but still everywhere. What am I?

134. What peels like an onion but still remains whole?

135. When is it bad luck to meet a white cat?

136. A farmer has 20 sheep, 10 pigs, and 10 cows. If we call the pigs cows, how many cows will he have?

137. As clear as diamonds, polished like glass. Try to keep me, and I vanish fast. What am I?

138. I soar without wings; I see without eyes. I traveled the universe and live where dreams lie. I've conquered the world, yet I'm always home. My ideas are untamed but want to be grown. What am I?

139. I am not alive, yet I can stand up. I begin as one color and then change rather abrupt. So fragile, a child could break one, yet strong enough to hold a horse's ton. What am I?

140. Break me and I get better, immediately harder to break again. What am I?

141. The sun bakes them. The hand takes them. The foot treads on them. The mouth tastes them. What are they?

142. I come in darkness and never when you call. I bring enlightenment to some, while tapping the emotions of all. What am I?

143. Some people hide me, but I will show. No matter how hard people try, never down will I go. What am I?

144. The strangest creature you'll ever find: two eyes in front and many more behind. What am I?

6

THIS ONE TIME. . . .

A man in a movie theater notices a grasshopper sitting in the next row. He leans forward and says, "Are you a grasshopper?" The grasshopper turns and looks at him and says, "Yes." The man responds, "What are you doing at the movies?" The grasshopper replies, "Well, I like the book!"

A penguin walks into a store, goes to the counter, and says to the cashier, "Have you seen my brother?" The cashier says, "I don't know. What does he look like?"

My teachers told me I'd never amount to much because I procrastinate. I told them, "Just you wait!"

Vincent listens intently when his chemistry teacher looks at the periodic table and says, "Oxygen is a must for breathing and life. It was discovered in 1773." Vincent shakes his head and calls out, "Well, it's a good thing I was born after 1773!"

"Jane," the teacher asked, "What is the formula for water?" Jane thought for a minute and replied, "H, I, J, K, L, M, N, O." "No, Jane, that's supposed to be H-2-O." Jane shook her head. "That's what I said!"

Two cupcakes are in the oven baking together when one of them says, "Gee, if we don't get out of here alive, I just want to say, I love you." The other cupcake says, "Oh my gosh . . . A talking cupcake!"

A man runs into a hospital emergency room screaming, "Help me! I'm shrinking!" A nurse grabs him and sits the man down in the waiting room. "We're very busy here today, sir, you're going to have to be a little patient."

A young boy knocks on a door on Halloween night and says, "Trick or treat?" A woman opens the door, looks at him, and says, "I don't know if I can give you a treat. What are you supposed to be?" The boy pauses and answers, "A werewolf." The woman shakes her head. "But you're not wearing a costume!" With a laugh, the boy replies, "Well, it's not a full moon yet, is it?"

Shannon just got her license and drove to school. She walked in to class well after the late bell rang. The teacher looked up at her and demanded, "Why are you so late?" Shannon explained, "Because of the traffic sign." The teacher shook her head and asked, "What traffic sign?" Shannon pointed outside. "Look. The sign that says, 'School Ahead Drive Slow.'"

Cameron was planting flower seeds on a hot day, sweating from the bright sun. He wiped his brow and said, "I'm so hot." His neighbor said, "You need to wait until the sun goes down, or plant in the morning when it is coolest." Cameron said, "I can't do that. It says on the package, 'Plant in full sun!'"

A lifeguard stormed up to Aiden's mother angrily. "Tell Aiden to stop peeing in the pool!" he demanded. The mother shrugged indifferently. "Everyone knows that from time to time, young children will urinate in the pool," the mother lectured him. "Oh really?" the angry lifeguard sneered. "From the diving board?!"

Simon handed his mom a beautifully wrapped box with a birthday surprise in it. She opened it up and said, "Oh, Simon, what a pretty teapot." Simon asked eagerly, "Do you like it?" "It's lovely," she replied. "But I have a rather nice one already." Simon gulped. "Umm . . . No, you don't."

Malcolm and his mother were at the supermarket and had a long discussion about where milk comes from. The whole ride home, Malcolm was quiet. "Is everything okay, Malcolm?" his mother asked. "Yes. I'm just thinking," he replied. "What are you thinking about?" she asked. "Mama, how do cows sit on all of those little bottles?"

A father frantically called the doctor. "Doctor, doctor, my son grabbed my pen and swallowed it. What do I do?" The doctor took a deep breath and replied, "Use another one until I get there."

Frizzik the cannibal was late for dinner again. His wife, Annabul, was really angry. This was the third time in a week! Annabul's mother sat at the table chewing on a bone. The old lady grumbled, "Just give him the cold shoulder when he gets here."

A guy is walking through the woods one day when he comes across a suitcase. He takes a look inside, only to find a fox and her cubs. He calls the animal authorities and tells the woman who answers the phone what he's found. She says, "Oh, that's horrible. Are they moving?" The guy replies, "I don't know, but that would explain the suitcase."

There are special schools popping up everywhere. If you're a surfer, maybe you'll go to Boarding School. Giants have a preference for High School. King Arthur went to Knight School. The ice-cream man got his degree from Sundae School.

An elephant drinking from a stream sees a tortoise lounging on the shore. He grabs it with his trunk and flings it into the jungle. A passing zebra asked, "Why'd you do that?" The elephant said, "Forty years ago that very tortoise bit my tail just for fun." Shocked, the zebra exclaimed, "Wow, forty years ago! How'd you remember that?" To which the elephant replied, "Well, I have turtle recall."

Two cows are standing in a field eating grass. The first cow turns to the second and says, "Moooooo!" The second cow replies, "Hey, I was just about to say the same thing!"

Carl asks his mom if he can have some animal crackers. His mom gives him a box of crackers and tells him he can just have a few. His mom leaves and comes back in a few minutes, finding all the crackers on the floor with Carl looking through them. His mother asks, "What are you doing, Carl?" Carl replies, "It said, 'Don't eat if the seal is already broken.' But I can't find a seal!"

A man walks into a seafood store carrying a salmon under his arm. "Hey, do you make fish cakes?" he asks. "Yes, we do," replies the fishmonger. "Great," says the man. "It's his birthday."

A man walks into a shop and sees a cute little dog. He asks the shopkeeper, "Does your dog bite?" The shopkeeper says, "No, my dog doesn't bite." The man reaches down to pet the dog and the dog bites him. "Ouch!" the man says. "I thought you said your dog doesn't bite!" The shopkeeper replies, "That's not my dog!"

Mr. and Mrs. Jones have two children. One is named Mind Your Own Business and the other is named Trouble. On the first day of school, the two kids decided to play hide-and-seek while at recess. Trouble hid while Mind Your Own Business counted to one hundred. Mind Your Own Business began looking for her brother behind hidden corners, the slide, and bushes. The bell rang ending recess and neither child got in line to reenter the school. Mind Your Own Business kept looking despite the lunch aide calling for her to get on the line. The aide approached her and asked, "What are you doing?" "Playing a game," the girl replied. "What is your name?" the aide questioned. "Mind Your Own Business." Furious, the aide inquired, "Are you looking for trouble?!" The girl looked up and replied, "Yes!"

A fly feels a bug on its back and asks, "Hey, bug on my back, are you a mite?" "I mite be," giggles the mite. "That's the worst pun I've ever heard," the fly groans. "What do you expect?" asks the mite. "I came up with it on the fly."

....

Grandma was babysitting little Eric. She had a stack of coins on the table and when she came into the room, they were missing. "Eric! Where are the coins?" Eric pointed to his mouth and said, "Yum." Grandma called her daughter and rushed her grandson to the hospital. Eric's parents met her there and took Eric into the emergency room. Grandma sat in the waiting room, watching the clock. An hour passed, then two. She was nervous. Grandma knocked on the glass window. "I just want to know how my grandson is doing." The attendant said she'd get the nurse. A minute later the nurse appeared. "How's Eric?" The nurse shook her head. "No change yet."

One day a fly is buzzing around a wolfhound and decides to ask him, "What kind of dog are you?" The dog replies, "I'm a wolfhound." The fly says, "A wolfhound? That's an odd name. Why do they call you that?" The dog says, "Well, it's quite simple, really. My mother was a hound, and my dad was a wolf." The fly replies, "Oh, I see . . ." Then the dog asks the fly, "So, what kind of fly are you?" The fly says, "I'm a horsefly." To which the dog says, "NOOO WAAAAYYYYY!!!"

A woman owned a rabbit farm and was known around the world for her rabbits who could lift more than any man. Wanting to start her own rabbit farm, Hallie decided she must see these rabbits. She took the train to see them. It was a long trip, but she knew if she wanted to pursue her dream of a rabbit farm, she'd have to see this one. The farmer met Hallie at the station and took her in her truck to see the farm. Sure enough, there were hundreds of rabbits. They were moving boulders with their noses. Some stood on their hind legs and were pushing wheelbarrows filled with produce. "I've never seen anything like this!" Hallie exclaimed. "Look at these rabbits; they are the strongest I've ever seen!" The farmer beamed with pride. Hallie turned to her. "You must tell me your secret. You must!" she implored. "Well," the farmer said. "It's really no secret." She reached into the pocket of her overalls and pulled out a bottle of shampoo. She pointed to the label, where in big letters it stated, "Keeps your hare strong."

Omar broke both his arms in an accident. He wore a cast on each of them from wrist to elbow. They were propped up by a big bar that held them aloft. He took a walk and paused outside a music shop. In the window was the most beautiful guitar he had ever seen. He stared at it for a long time, shook his head, and walked in the door. "How much is that guitar?" He nodded toward the instrument. "That one?" the store owner said. "It's very expensive." Omar responded, "That's all right. I'd like to buy it." The owner looked at the guitar and then back to the two casts holding up Omar's arms. "And how, may I ask, do you intend to play it?" Omar smiled. "I'll just play it by ear."

Mrs. Jackson is announcing her class's next speaker for career day, who happens to be a butcher. She says, "He has chicken wings, pig cheeks, and chicken thighs." Shocked, one of the students says, "He must be really funny looking."

A businessperson was driving down a country road when he spotted a little boy with a lemonade stand. It was hot and he was thirsty, so he decided to stop. Once he got up to the little boy's stand, he noticed a sign that said, "All-you-can-drink 10 cents," and a single, very small glass. Well, he thought that it was an awfully small glass, but since it was only a dime for all-you-can-drink, he decided to get some anyway. He gave the boy a dime and gulped down the lemonade in one swig. He slapped the glass back onto the table and said, "Fill 'er up." The kid replied, "Sure thing, that'll be 10 cents more." The businessperson said, "But your sign says, 'All-you-can-drink 10 cents.'" The little boy replied, "That's right. That's all you can drink for 10 cents."

This dog walks into a telegraph office and picks up a blank form. He writes on it, "Woof. Woof. Woof. Woof. Woof. Woof. Woof. Woof. Woof." Then he hands the form to the clerk. The clerk looks it over and says, "You know, there are only nine words here. You could add another 'Woof' for the same price." The dog shakes his head at the clerk in disbelief and says, "But then it would make no sense at all."

Two friends are walking their dogs, a Boxer and a Chihuahua, when they smell a delicious aroma coming from a nearby restaurant. The guy with the Boxer says, "Let's get something to eat." The guy with the Chihuahua replies, "We can't go in there, we have dogs with us. They are not allowed." The first guy says, "Just follow my lead." He puts on a pair of sunglasses and walks into the restaurant. "Sorry," the owner says, stopping him. "No pets allowed." "This is my Seeing Eye dog," the guy with the Boxer says. "A Boxer?" the owner asks. "Yes, they're using them now." The owner says, "Very well, then, come on in." The guy with the Chihuahua repeats the process and gets the same response from the owner: "Sorry, no pets allowed." "But this is my Seeing Eye dog," says the second guy. "A Chihuahua?" asks the owner. "A Chihuahua?!" says the man in the dark glasses. "They gave me a Chihuahua?!"

Tim points to a dog walking past him on the street. "Do you see that dog?" he says to his friend Ralphie. "Yeah, what about him?" Ralphie asks. Tim responds, "He went to the flea circus and stole the show!"

Mrs. Beaks decided to teach a lesson on logical thinking. "This is the scene," said the teacher.

"A man is standing up in a boat in the middle of a river, fishing. He loses his balance, falls in, and begins splashing and yelling for help. His wife hears him, knows he can't swim, and runs down to the bank. Why do you think she ran to the bank?" One girl raises her hand proudly and asks, "To withdraw his savings?"

Two brothers, Charley and Ron, are trying to start a farm. Charley finds a prized bull in the ads and leaves to check it out. He tells Ron that he will contact him to come haul the bull back to the farm if he buys it. Charley goes to the farm and loves the bull. He decides to buy it. The farmer tells him that the bull will cost exactly $599, no less. So, Charley buys the bull and heads to town to contact Ron. The only person he can find to help him is a telegraph operator. The operator tells him, "It costs 99 cents per word. What would you like to send?" Charley replies, "Well I only have $1.00 left." He thinks for a while and tells the operator he wants to send the word "comfortable." The operator asks, "How will he know you bought the bull and want him to bring the truck from the word 'comfortable'?" Charley states, "He's a slow reader."

A man believes he is a mouse and finally goes to a doctor to get help. After some weeks of counseling, he is finally healed and has learned that he isn't a mouse after all. As the man walks out of the doctor's office, he sees a cat on the street and runs back in the office screaming, "I'm scared! There's a cat on the street!" The doctor replies, "I thought you understood now that you are not a mouse." To which the man answers, "Yes, but does the cat know that?"

An antiques dealer is walking through town and sees a cat drinking milk from a saucer in a shop window. He does a double take. The saucer is very rare. He is shocked when he realizes that the saucer is an expensive find. He must have it. He enters the shop and asks the owner, "Hey, I really like that cat. Would you be willing to sell it to me?" The store owner replies, "Not for sale." The antiques dealer, thinking quickly, responds, "I'll give you $200 for it!" The shop owner agrees, and the antiques dealer grabs the cat. He acts like he is about to leave, but then adds, "Oh, would you mind throwing in the saucer? The cat seems to like it." The shop owner replies, "No way! That's my lucky saucer. I've sold hundreds of cats since I got it."

This guy gets a parrot, but it's got a grumpy attitude. The owner tries everything to change the bird's attitude, but nothing works. Finally, in a moment of desperation, he puts the parrot in the freezer. For a few moments he hears the bird squawking, and then, suddenly, all is quiet. He opens the freezer door. The parrot steps out and says, "I'm sorry that I offended you with my actions. I ask for your forgiveness." The guy is shocked by the bird's change in attitude and is about to ask what caused the transformation when the parrot continues, "By the way, may I ask, what did the chicken do?"

Two boys, Michael and Rob, walk into a candy store. While in the store, Michael steals five candy bars and puts them in his pocket. When the boys leave, Michael brags, "I stole five candy bars, beat that!" Rob says, "No problem, just follow me." They go back into the store and Rob goes up to one of the shopkeepers. He asks the shopkeeper, "Would you like to see some magic, sir?" The man says yes, and Rob immediately opens five candy bars and eats them as fast as he can. The shopkeeper, who is now angry, demands, "Where is the magic?" Rob replies, "Ta-da! The candy bars are now in my friend's pockets."

A guy was driving past a farm one day when he noticed a beautiful horse standing in one of the fields. Hoping to buy the horse, the guy stopped and offered the farmer $500 for it. The farmer said, "Sorry, he's not for sale. He doesn't look too good." The guy said, "He looks just fine. Tell you what, I'll give you $1,000 for him." The farmer again said, "Sorry, he's not for sale. He doesn't look too good." The guy now really wanted the horse and so increased his offer to $1,500. The farmer said, "Well, he doesn't look so good, but if you want him that much, he's yours." So, the guy bought the horse and took him home. The next day he returned to the farm, furious with the farmer. The man jumped out of his car to shout at the farmer calmly raking the hay, "Hey, you cheated me! You sold me a blind horse!" The farmer looked up and responded, "I told you he didn't look too good."

A grocer puts up a sign above his turkeys, "$5 each or $20 for three." All day long, people approach him, outraged by his incorrect math, and say, "It should be $15 for three; I'll just buy three turkeys separately then." After one of his employees watches this go on all day, he asks him, "Are you going to fix the sign or what?" The grocer laughs, "Why should I stop a good thing? Before I put up the sign nobody ever bought three turkeys."

A panda walks into a diner and the diner owner decides to let him stay. The panda eats his dinner and then asks for the check. He looks at the check, nods, shoots the waiter in the knee, and leaves the restaurant. The boss runs over and looks at the table. The panda left behind an open dictionary, turned to the page with the word "panda" on it. The boss reads the description: "Panda; n. Large mammal. Eats shoots and leaves."

A young girl peeks over the counter and politely says to the sales representative, "I'm interested in buying a rabbit." The saleswoman gushes, "Oh sure, sweetie. Do you have any specific color in mind? We've got some adorable white bunnies down this aisle." The girl waves her hand. "I really don't think my boa constrictor will care what color it is!"

Lloyd goes into a pet shop and tells the owner that he needs a pet for his mother. He says that his mom lives alone and could really use some company. The pet shop owner says, "I have just what she needs: a parrot that can speak five languages. She'll be very entertained by that bird." Lloyd says he'll take the parrot and makes arrangements to have the bird delivered to his mom. A few days pass and Lloyd calls his mother. "Well, Mom, how did you like that bird I sent?" She says, "Oh, Son, he was delicious!" Shocked, Lloyd says, "Mom, you ate that bird? He could speak five languages!" His mom responds, "Well, he should have said something!"

A man has always had the dream of being in a circus. He approaches the manager of the circus and tells him, "I can do the best bird impression you have ever seen." The manager says, "That's nothing special, a lot of people can do bird impressions." The man turns and says, "Okay." Then he starts to flap his arms and flies away.

An old man went to the doctor complaining of a terrible pain in his leg. "I am afraid it's just old age," the doctor replied. "There is nothing we can do about it." The old man fumed, "That can't be! You don't know what you are doing." The doctor countered, "How can you possibly know that I am wrong?" The old man replied, "Well, it's quite obvious. My other leg is fine and it's the exact same age!"

Martin received his brand-new driver's license. The family gathered on the driveway, climbed in the car, and asked where he was going to take them for a ride for the first time. The dad immediately headed for the back seat, directly behind the new driver. "I'll bet you're back there to get a change of scenery after all those months in the front passenger seat, teaching me how to drive," says the beaming boy to his father. "Nope," his dad replied. "I'm gonna sit here and kick the back of your seat as you drive, just like you've been doing to me all these years."

Three men are traveling through the desert. They are very thirsty. They come to a mysterious waterslide in the middle of the desert that has these words written at the top: "Slide down and yell the drink of your choice. At the bottom you will find a pool of that beverage." The three men are very excited. The first man slides down and yells, "Water!" and falls into a pool of water. The next man goes down and yells, "Lemonade!" and falls into a pool full of refreshing lemonade. The final man goes down and, overwhelmed with excitement, yells, "Weeee!"

A couple walks into a hole-in-the-wall restaurant. As they're about to sit down, they notice crumbs on the seat, so they wipe down the booth and table. A waitress comes over asking what they want. "I'll take a coffee," the man says. "Me too," the woman replies, "and make sure the cup is clean." The waitress returns with their drinks and places down their cups. "Now, which one of you wanted the clean cup?"

Clyde strode into John's stable looking to buy a horse. "Listen here," said John. "I've got just the horse you're looking for. The only thing is, he was trained by a strange fellow. He doesn't stop and go in the usual way. When you need to stop you must scream 'Hey-hey.' The way to get him to move is to say 'Thank Goodness.'" Clyde nodded and thought that was easy enough. "Well, I need a horse. Fine with me. Can I take him for a test run?" he asked. John nodded. He reminded him about the weird commands and slapped the back of the horse, sending Clyde down the road. Clyde was having the time of his life. This horse could run! Clyde was galloping down the dirt road when he suddenly saw a cliff up ahead. "Stop!" he screamed, but the horse kept on going. He pulled at the reins, but the horse didn't even slow down. Not one bit. No matter how much he tried, he could not remember the words to get it to stop. "Yo-yo!" he shouted. Still, the horse just kept on speeding straight to the end of the road. He was going to fall down the steep cliff! Clyde and the horse were five feet from the cliff when Clyde suddenly remembered the right command. "Hey-hey!" he shouted as loud as he could. The horse skidded to a halt just inches from the edge of the cliff. Clyde could not believe his good luck. He looked up to the sky, breathed a deep sigh of relief, and said, "Thank Goodness."

Riddle Answers

1. An elephant's shadow!

2. A hole.

3. A telephone.

4. Short.

5. He's alive.

6. A goose.

7. A rhinoceros.

8. An automobile.

9. A tennis ball.

10. A coat of paint.

11. A flag.

12. A relationship.

13. Neither, they both burn shorter!

14. A scale.

15. A stamp.

16. Because all his uncles are ants.

17. A horse.

18. Wrong.

19. Eight. Horses have hooves and chickens have claws. Only the four humans, the farmer and his family, have feet.

20. He is walking.

21. The president.

22. Your voice.

23. Stars.

24. It wasn't raining.

25. Because the batteries died.

26. A shadow.

27. "O I C U R M T."

28. The letter "m."

29. Pilgrims.

30. Gold.

31. Just fine. People have fingers on both hands!

32. She was born on February 29, in a leap year!

33. A deck of cards.

34. A battery.

35. The match.

36. Plates.

37. A reflection.

38. A feather.

39. A cowboy riding his horse.

40. Because it has four eyes but it cannot see!

41. An umbrella.

42. "Alphabet."

43. Legs.

44. The word "ton."

45. The letter "g."

46. Footsteps.

47. The one with the biggest head.

48. None. He has three sisters.

49. Three.

50. She fell from the bottom step.

51. A street.

52. A catcher and an umpire.

53. "Underground."

54. Money.

55. Age.

56. A pillow.

57. Rain.

Bonus Math Riddle 1:
$888 + 88 + 8 + 8 + 8 = 1000$.

58. The letter "D."

59. The alphabet.

60. Misspelled!

61. A deal.

62. A shadow.

63. Three: one blonde, one brunette, and one redhead.

64. An address.

65. "NOON."

66. A tree.

67. A brain.

68. A mirror.

69. A straw-berry.

70. A tree.

71. "Few."

72. Thunder.

73. "Queue."

74. A mirror.

75. Charcoal.

76. A key.

77. When it's frozen.

78. The letter "k."

79. A promise.

80. A book.

81. "Empty."

82. A shoe.

83. A cabbage.

84. Your word.

85. The moon.

86. A lightbulb.

87. A pillow.

88. Ohio.

89. Your finger.

90. Edam.

91. C-A-T.

92. A refrigerator.

93. A flight of stairs.

94. The sun.

95. A football match.

96. A brook.

97. A mirror.

98. A match.

99. A deck of cards.

100. A shirt.

101. The letter "L."

102. A stapler.

103. Sawdust.

104. A pen.

105. Day and night.

106. A dictionary.

107. A compass.

108. A snowman.

109. Eyes.

110. A nest.

111. A snake.

Bonus Math Riddle 2: The answer has to do with time! If 11:00 a.m. plus two hours is 1:00 p.m., then 9:00 p.m. plus five hours is 2:00 a.m.

112. A fish.

113. It churned the cream to make butter!

114. The chain was not attached to anything!

115. A bowling ball knocked down 10 pins!

116. A book!

117. A coin.

118. A feather.

119. Nothing.

120. The ocean.

121. A cherry.

122. She is reading braille.

123. An icicle.

124. They only sleep at night.

125. Zero seconds. The house was already built by the first 20 people!

126. A broom.

127. Corn.

128. Eat. (ate)

129. Cubes only have six sides.

130. Neither, the yolks of eggs are yellow.

131. No, because he is already dead.

132. A queen bee.

133. Lightning

134. A lizard.

135. When you're a mouse.

136. Ten. (We can call the pigs cows, but that doesn't make them cows.)

137. Ice.

138. Imagination.

139. Human hair.

140. A world record.

141. Grapes.

142. A dream.

143. Age.

144. A peacock.

Build Your Own Comedy Library

365 Jokes for Kids: A Joke A Day Book by Chrissy Voeg

Knock, Knock! Who's There?
My First Book of Knock-Knock Jokes by Tad Hills

Silly Jokes for Silly Kids by Silly Willy

A Whole Lotta Knock-Knock Jokes: Squeaky-Clean Family Fun by Mike Spohr and Heather Spohr

The Big Book of

Tricky Riddles for Kids

400+ RIDDLES!

Corinne Schmitt

Illustrations by Dylan Goldberger

For Mr. Byer, my fourth grade
teacher, who introduced me
to the joy of riddles.

Contents

Riddle
Me This

Riddles are a fun way to exercise your brain. They're simple questions that require a bit of clever thinking to answer, letting you practice lots of helpful skills like critical thinking, deductive reasoning, attention to detail, creativity, and problem solving. You'll also learn to be patient and persistent, since the answer to a riddle usually isn't obvious.

There are lots of different types of riddles. This book has everything from clever one-liners to challenging brain teasers—and some silly riddles for extra fun. Some answers are on the same page, so you can make a game of it by challenging friends and family. Or you can cover the answers and tackle them yourself!

You may find you have a knack for specific types of riddles, while others take more effort. That's what makes riddles so great! You'll learn some unique ways to think—and have fun doing it.

Let's start riddling!

1

Clever Qs & Crafty As

Riddles have been around for thousands of years. The very first recorded riddle is from Mesopotamia in 2350 BCE (find this ancient riddle at the end of the chapter). For centuries, people all over the world have enjoyed trying to stump one another with riddles. Why? Like most other things we do for fun, riddles help distract our minds, and they give us an opportunity to stretch our brains. Just like sports let us practice physical skills, riddles let us practice mental skills. But unlike a game of soccer or basketball, you don't need a large group of people to solve a riddle.

Ready to start having some fun with riddles? This chapter is full of short one-liners with answers that are just as brief. But don't be fooled! You'll find many of these are pretty tricky, so you'll have to think hard—and creatively—to solve them.

1. If you take two apples from three apples, how many do you have?

Two, because that is how many you took. (Told you they're tricky!)

2. How can you stand behind your father while he is standing behind you?

By standing back to back.

3. What has two hands but cannot scratch its face?

A clock.

4. If Sam's parents have three sons and the first two are Huey and Dewey, what is the third son's name?

Sam.

5. In a one-story red house with red walls, red carpet, and red doors, what color are the stairs?

There are no stairs in a one-story house.

6. Which letter comes next in this sequence: M, T, W, T, F, S?

S; the letters are the first letters of each day of the week.

7. If a man stood out in the pouring rain without an umbrella, hat, hood, or canopy over him, but his hair did not get wet, how was it possible?

He's bald.

8. Name two days that start with the letter T besides Tuesday and Thursday.

Today and tomorrow.

9. What kind of room can you eat?

A mushroom.

10. What are two things you can never have for breakfast?

Lunch and dinner.

11. Can a kangaroo jump higher than a mountain?

Of course, because mountains can't jump.

12. Which month of the year has 28 days?

They all do; no month has fewer than 28 days.

13. What can be measured but cannot be seen, taken but not given, and told but not heard?

Time.

14. What five-letter word do even the smartest people pronounce wrong?

The word *wrong*.

15. If two mothers and two daughters go to the store and each buys a new purse, why do they only bring home three purses?

Because there are only three people: a grandmother, her daughter, and her granddaughter.

16. If I have two coins that total 30 cents and one of them is not a quarter, what are the two coins?

A nickel *and* a quarter. If one is not a quarter, the other is!

17. Where does today come before yesterday?

In the dictionary.

18. What has 10 letters and starts with gas?

Automobile.

19. What are some things that can run but not walk?

Water, ink, paint, and noses!

20. When should you give gorilla milk to a baby?

When the baby is a gorilla.

21. How can two babies be born on the same day to the same mother and not be twins?

They are two of the three babies in triplets.

22. How many seconds are in a year?

There are 12: January 2nd, February 2nd, etc.

23. What honorable thing can you break without touching?

A promise.

24. What looks exactly like a cat but isn't a cat?

A picture of a cat or a cat's reflection in a mirror.

25. How can you drop an egg on a concrete floor without cracking it?

Easy—an egg will never crack a concrete floor.

26. A man jumped out of an airplane without a parachute and survived. How?

The plane was on the ground.

27. What food stays hot even if you put it in the refrigerator?

A jalapeño, because it's a hot pepper.

28. How many letters are there in the alphabet? (Hint: The answer is NOT 26!)

There are 11: three in "the" and eight in "alphabet."

> ### MIX IT UP
> This is a fun one to stump adults with. See if your family can figure it out without any clues. If they can't get it, let them ask yes-or-no questions to see if that helps.

29. When is it okay to go on red and stop on green?

When eating a watermelon.

30. How do you fix a broken pizza?

With tomato paste.

31. What type of shells do you never find in the ocean?

Dry shells.

32. Name a fruit whose letters can be rearranged to spell another fruit.

Lemon/melon.

33. Which burns longer: white candles or yellow candles?

Neither: candles burn shorter, not longer.

34. What kind of table can you eat?

A vegetable.

35. Which weighs more, a pound of bubble wrap or a pound of bricks?

Neither; they both weigh one pound.

36. What has a bottom at its top?

Legs.

37. Which two words, when put together, have the most letters?

Post office.

SILLY STATS

The US postal service delivers more than 180 million pieces of first-class mail every day! They process more than 5,000 pieces of mail every second.

---

38. What kind of tree can you carry in your hand?

Palm.

39. How do you make the number one disappear?

Add the letter G or N to the beginning so it is gone or none.

40. What three keys cannot open any locks?

Donkey, jockey, and monkey.

41. If you have five grapefruits in your left hand and another five in your right hand, what do you have?

Really big hands.

42. What belongs to you but is used more by other people?

Your name.

43. What can you put in a bag of grain to make it lighter and easier to carry?

A hole.

44. How is it possible to go 30 days without sleeping?

Only sleep at night.

SILLY STATS

The longest that we know any person has gone without sleep is about 11 days. If you want your brain to function at peak ability, it's important to get a good night's sleep each night!

45. Why is it that when something is lost, it's always found in the very last place you looked?

Because after you find it, you stop looking.

46. Why did the little boy stare at the can of juice?

Because it said, "Concentrate."

47. What common verb becomes past tense when you rearrange its letters?

Eat (ate).

48. How can you place a book on the floor so that no one can jump over it?

Lean it against the wall.

49. What do celebrities and air conditioners have in common?

They both have fans.

50. How many birthdays does an 80-year-old woman have?

One . . . everyone has only one *birthday*.

51. What type of band never plays music?

A rubber band.

52. What do you have to break before you can use it?

An egg.

53. Is a $20 bill from 1920 more valuable than a new one?

Yes, $20 is always more than one.

54. Is it ever correct to say, "I is" instead of "I am"?

Yes, when talking about the letter *I*, as in "*I* is the first letter in the word 'is.'"

MIX IT UP

This is another fun one to try on adults. If they answer no, assure them the answer is yes and see if they can come up with an example.

55. How is it that a woman is driving without her headlights on when there is no moon or streetlights, yet she can see a dog in the road ahead?

It is daytime.

56. Where is the ocean deepest?

At the bottom.

SILLY STATS

The deepest part of the Earth's surface is near the Philippines, in an area called the Mariana Trench. The location is referred to as "Challenger Deep." It is more than 36,000 feet below sea level. If you moved Mount Everest to the Challenger Deep, the tip of the mountain would still be more than a mile below the ocean's surface!

57. Name three states that contain no cities or counties.

Solid, liquid, and gas (the three states of matter).

58. What was the longest river in the world before the Amazon River was discovered?

The Amazon River was still the longest, it just had not been discovered yet.

59. Why does Jane, whose birthday is December 25, celebrate her birthday during the summer?

Because she lives in the southern hemisphere, where seasons are the opposite of those in the northern hemisphere.

60. If it takes seven minutes to boil an egg, how long does it take to boil one dozen eggs?

It still only takes seven minutes, since you can boil them all at once.

61. Who always sleeps with shoes on?

A horse.

62. Can the letters in NEW DOOR be rearranged to spell one word?

Yes, ONE WORD uses all the letters from NEW DOOR.

63. What's the name for a person who does not have all their fingers on one hand?

Typical—most people have all ten of their fingers on *two* hands (on one hand they only have half their fingers).

64. What question can you never honestly answer "yes"?

Are you asleep?

65. What four-letter word can be read left to right, even when written upside down or backward?

NOON.

66. What kind of bet can never be won?

An alphabet.

67. What has no hands but is able to build?

A bird.

> **AROUND THE WORLD**
>
> This is a riddle from the Russian tradition of household and barnyard riddles called загадки (pronounced "zagadki"). They're popular among fourth and fifth graders in Russia.

68. Stupendous is a tricky word. How do you spell it?

I-T.

69. What type of ship is not used to travel in water?

A friendship. Bonus points if you also thought of relationship!

70. Which word does not belong: red, orange, yellow, blue, green, or indigo?

Or.

71. Which is correct: My dog ate the largest half of my sandwich, or my dog ate the larger half of my sandwich?

Neither, because halves are the same size.

72. What is as large as an elephant but weighs nothing at all?

Its shadow.

73. How is it possible to have a room full of people, and yet there isn't a single person there?

Everyone is married.

74. What type of nut has a hole in the center?

A donut.

75. How can you throw a ball as hard as you can and still have it return to you without anyone or anything else touching it?

Throw it straight up in the air.

76. How do you make a line drawn on a piece of paper longer without touching the line?

Draw a shorter line beneath it, and the original line is now the longer of the two.

77. What kind of dress can never be worn?

An address.

78. How many pairs of pants can you put into an empty hamper?

None; as soon as you put anything in, it is not empty anymore.

79. What does a dog have that no other animal has?

Puppies.

80. If Isabella has three daughters and each daughter has a brother, how many children does she have?

Four; three daughters and one son.

81. Noah fell off a 40-foot ladder but did not get hurt. How?

He only fell from the bottom rung.

82. How can a leopard change its spots?

Move from one spot to another.

83. What word is pronounced the same even if you take away four of its letters?

Queue.

84. Will a stone fall faster in a pail of water that is 25 degrees Celsius or in a pail of water that is 25 degrees Fahrenheit?

In the pail of 25 degrees Celsius water since the other pail is frozen.

85. How many legs does an ant have if you call its antennae legs?

Six. Calling its antennae legs does not make them legs.

86. Without needing to know their meanings, what do the words *abstemiously*, *facetiously*, and *placentious* have in common?

They contain all five vowels in alphabetical order.

RIDDLE HISTORY

Abstemiously means that someone eats and drinks in moderation. (They don't overindulge.) *Facetiously* means that what has been said isn't meant to be taken seriously. Long ago, *placentious* was used to refer to a person who is likeable, but the word is no longer commonly used.

87. Why are ghosts such bad liars?

Because you can see right through them.

88. What kind of goose doesn't have feathers?

A mongoose.

89. What kind of ball can be rolled but not bounced or thrown?

An eyeball.

90. Which side of a dog has more fur?

The outside.

91. What two types of cups can you never drink from?

A hiccup and a cupcake.

92. If you throw a blue stone into the Red Sea, what will it become?

Wet.

93. There is a house. One enters it blind and comes out seeing. What is it? (Note: What is the house?)

A school.

RIDDLE HISTORY

This is the oldest known riddle. It was found engraved on a clay tablet found in ancient Mesopotamia (now Iraq). Kids 4,000 years ago enjoyed riddles as much as we do today!

2

WHAT AM I?

An *enigma* is something mysterious or difficult to figure out. In riddles, the term enigma describes puzzles that have hidden meanings. The questions are asked in a way that is meant to trick you on purpose.

This chapter is full of these kinds of enigmas. Each riddle will provide a brief description, written from the perspective of a specific person, place, or thing, followed by a simple question: "What am I?" They will be more cunning than the one-liners in chapter 1, as each one has been written with the specific goal of fooling you.

Don't worry, they're not too tricky! Try to think of alternative definitions of the words used in the riddles, and use some creative thinking. Once you've done a few, they'll get easier. These riddles are especially fun to figure out with others since different perspectives will help you look at the riddles from several angles.

94. I am weightless, but you can see me. Put me in a jug, and I will make it lighter. What am I?

A hole.

95. I am never quite what I appear to be. I seem simple, but only the wise understand me. What am I?

A riddle!

MIX IT UP

What other clues can you think of for "a riddle"? In chapter 7, I'll show you how to make up your own riddles, but this one is fun to practice on.

---

96. I am at the beginning of eternity and the end of time. What am I?

The letter e.

97. I move quickly but do not have feet. You can hear me, but I do not have a mouth. What am I?

The wind.

98. The more I dry, the wetter I get. What am I?

A towel.

99. I have branches but no leaves or bark. What am I?

A library.

100. I have rivers but no water, cities but no buildings, roads but no cars. What am I?

A map.

101. I taste better than I smell. What am I?

A tongue.

102. I am so fragile that if you say my name, I break. What am I?

Silence.

103. I shave facial hair every day but am still able to grow an exceptionally long beard. What am I?

A barber.

104. I always reply but have no mouth. What am I?

An echo.

105. The more you take away from me, the larger I get. What am I?

A hole.

106. I am always in front of you, but you cannot see me. What am I?

The future.

107. You can only keep me after giving me to someone else. What am I?

Your word or promise.

108. I have many keys but cannot open a single lock. What am I?

A piano.

109. You can hold me in your right hand but never in your left hand. What am I?

Your left elbow.

110. I have one head, one foot, and four legs. What am I?

A bed.

111. Forward I am heavy, but backward I am not. What am I?

The word "ton."

112. I can go up but can never come down. What am I?

Your age.

113. I am taller when I am sitting than when I am standing. What am I?

A dog.

AROUND THE WORLD

Riddles like these, along with proverbs, are common in Africa, where people use them to share wisdom about things they observe in life and nature.

114. I can only live in light but disappear if light shines directly on me. What am I?

A shadow.

115. I am not alive, but I can die. What am I?

A battery.

116. I fly all day but have no wings and never leave my spot. What am I?

A flag.

117. I have a neck but no head, and yet I wear a cap. What am I?

A bottle.

118. I am a seed whose name is three letters long and pronounced the same even when you remove the last two letters. What am I?

A pea.

119. I come alive when I am buried but perish when I'm dug up. What am I?

A plant.

120. I have many ears but cannot hear. What am I?

A cornfield.

121. You can catch me, but you cannot throw me. What am I?

A cold.

122. I am easy to get into but hard to get out of. What am I?

Trouble.

123. I run all around the backyard, but I never move. What am I?

A fence.

124. I am a six-letter word found in many rooms. My first half is an automobile, my last half is a domesticated animal, and my first four letters are a type of fish. What am I?

Carpet.

125. I can build castles and break down mountains. I can blind you yet also help you see. What am I?

Sand.

SILLY STATS

Did you know sand can be used to make eyeglass lenses? Sand won't melt until it reaches 3090°F, so they're using some pretty amazing ovens to make glass from liquid sand!

126. I am always on the table at mealtime, but you do not get to eat me. What am I?

A plate.

127. I have many teeth but cannot bite, chew, or cut. What am I?

A comb.

128. I am black when you buy me, orange when you use me, and gray when you are done with me. What am I?

Charcoal.

129. If you lose me, the people around you will often lose me too. What am I?

Your temper.

130. You see me come down but never go up. What am I?

Rain.

131. I go up and down, but I never move. What am I?

A staircase, or temperature.

132. I am a building with more than 500 stories. What am I?

A library.

133. I am a fruit, a bird, and a person. What am I?

Kiwi.

AROUND THE WORLD

New Zealanders are affectionately referred to as Kiwis due to their admiration for the bird that has become their national symbol. It refers to their pleasant attitude and unique heritage.

134. I am not alive, but I need air and can grow. What am I?

A fire.

135. I have a bed, but I never sleep. I have a mouth, but I never eat. What am I?

A river.

136. I have three feet but cannot walk. What am I?

A yardstick.

137. I can fall out of a building and live, but if you put me in fire or water, I will die. What am I?

Paper.

138. I can be cracked, played, and made. What am I?

A joke.

139. I am a number with five letters in my name that appear in alphabetical order. What am I?

Forty.

140. I occur once in a minute, twice in a moment, but never in a thousand years. What am I?

The letter *m*.

141. Why can a man living in Canada not be buried in the United States?

Because he is still living.

142. The more you take of me, the more you leave behind. What am I?

Steps.

143. I have a thumb and four fingers, but I am not a hand. What am I?

A glove.

144. I can fill a room, but I take up no space. What am I?

Light. And laughter!

145. The faster you run, the harder it is to catch me. What am I?

Your breath.

146. I have keys but no doors, space but no rooms, and you can enter but you cannot leave. What am I?

A keyboard.

147. The more there is of me, the less you see. What am I?

Darkness.

148. I have four eyes but cannot see. What am I?

The word Mississippi.

149. What is easy to lift but hard to throw?

A feather.

150. I am noisy when I am changing. After I have changed, I am larger but weigh less. What am I?

Popcorn.

151. You can hold me, but not with your hands. You can bury me, but not underground. What am I?

A grudge or secret.

152. I make two people out of one. What am I?

A mirror.

153. When I am dirty, I am white, but when I am clean, I am green or black. What am I?

A chalkboard.

154. I am an insect. The first half of my name is the name of another insect. What am I?

A beetle.

155. No matter how much rain falls on me, I can never get wetter. What am I?

Water.

156. You throw me out when you need me but bring me in when you do not. What am I?

An anchor.

157. I sometimes run, but I cannot walk. You follow me everywhere. What am I?

Your nose.

158. I am often needed and given, but rarely taken. What am I?

Advice.

159. I come in many shapes, sizes, and colors. I look like I can fit in several different places, but I require one specific place. What am I?

A puzzle piece.

160. I am always in charge and never in debt. I am also the first of my kind. What am I?

The letter a.

161. I grow instantly larger in light and, just as quickly, get smaller in the dark. What am I?

The pupil of an eye.

162. What is at the end of a rainbow that isn't a color?

The letter w.

163. I have been around for thousands of years, but I am never more than one month old. What am I?

The moon.

AROUND THE WORLD

This is a popular Chinese lantern riddle. The term "lantern riddle" comes from the tradition of writing the riddles on the lanterns used in the Chinese Lantern Festival, which occurs every year on the 15th day of the first month of the Chinese lunar calendar.

164. I am the creator of invention and the maker of all adventure. What am I?

Curiosity.

165. I go in circles but travel straight. What am I?

A wheel.

166. I do not have feet, hands, legs, arms, or wings, yet I can crawl under doors or fly high into the sky. What am I?

Smoke.

167. You can take my whole away from me, but I will still have some left. What am I?

The word *wholesome*.

168. I am tall when I am young and short when I'm old. What am I?

A candle.

169. You answer me even though I never ask questions. What am I?

A phone, doorbell, or knock at the door.

170. I always have one eye open. What am I?

A needle.

171. I am light as a feather, but the strongest person in the world cannot hold me for five minutes. What am I?

Your breath.

172. Forward, I am something people do each day. Backward, I am something to fear. What am I?

Live.

173. We can be helpful or hurtful. You can hear us, but you cannot see us or touch us. What are we?

Words.

174. You can serve me, but I cannot be eaten. What am I?

A tennis ball or volleyball.

175. I travel from here to there by appearing, and back from there to here by disappearing. What am I?

The letter *t*.

176. You see me once in October, three times in December, but never in July or August. What am I?

The letter *e*.

177. You can see me but never touch or feel me. No matter how fast you approach me, I am always the same distance away. What am I?

The horizon.

178. I am small, white, and round and served at a table. Either two or four people can enjoy me, but I am never eaten. What am I?

A ping-pong ball.

179. I live on a busy street. When you visit me, it is always to see someone else, so I charge you rent. What am I?

A parking meter.

180. My first half is in the present, my second half in the past. I go up and down but never wander. What am I?

A seesaw.

181. I have two arms and two feet but no fingers or toes. I can carry things easily if my feet do not touch the ground. What am I?

A wheelbarrow.

182. I am always with you, yet you always leave me behind. What am I?

Fingerprints.

183. When I am yours, you can touch me but cannot see me. I can be thrown out but not thrown away. What am I?

A back.

184. I am made of wood but cannot be cut or broken. What am I?

Sawdust.

185. I can be thin but not fat. You consume me but cannot hold me. I am best fresh. What am I?

Air.

186. I build silver bridges and golden crowns. Who am I?

A dentist.

187. Even though I am told what to do at night and reliably do so the next morning, I am often grumbled at and always told to be quiet. What am I?

An alarm clock.

188. I had a bright start but could not take the pressure. I consume everything, but I do not eat anything. What am I?

A black hole.

189. I have a head but no body and leaves but no branches. What am I?

Lettuce.

190. I start sounding like I work for the CIA, then my middle is the middle of middle, and my end is the most-used section of the hospital. What creature am I?

A spider.

MIX IT UP

This one's a little unfair, because you may not have learned it yet. Try recruiting the help of someone a little older. (Hint: Someone who has taken seventh-grade science.)

RIDDLE HISTORY

Did you recognize this riddle? It's changed up a little, but based on the riddle the Sphinx posed to Harry Potter in *Harry Potter and the Goblet of Fire*.

BRAIN BENDER

191. I have many names spelled many ways, but I always have two Xs. What am I?

A woman (with two X chromosomes).

3

PUNS & JOKES

Have you ever heard of a *conundrum?* While some people use the term to describe a difficult problem, it can also be used to describe a riddle that involves a play on words. These types of riddles usually involve *puns.* Puns take advantage of the multiple meanings of a word or draw connections between words that sound similar. Some answers include similar-sounding words, like *please* or *peas* instead of *peace.*

Conundrums are typically meant to be funny, but they're also really tricky. You'll need to put on your thinking cap to make sense of the punny business in this chapter!

192. What bird is with you at breakfast, lunch, and dinner?

A swallow.

193. What did the angry cake say to the fork?

You want a piece of me?

194. What type of bone will a dog never eat?

A trombone.

195. What kind of lion never roars?

A dandelion.

196. What do you call an alligator in a vest?

An investigator.

197. What is fast, crunchy, and can travel far?

A rocket chip.

198. What did the quartz say to the geologist?

Don't take me for granite.

199. Why did the eighth grader bring a ladder to class?

Because she wanted to be in high school.

200. Why did the students eat their homework?

Because the teacher said it was a piece of cake.

201. What did the left eye say to the right eye?

Between you and me, something smells.

202. What do you call a cow that has had a baby?

De-calf-einated.

203. Why shouldn't you start a conversation with pi?

Because it goes on and on forever.

204. How did the rabbit travel?

By hare plane.

205. Why was the jalapeño wearing a sweater?

Because it was a little chile (chilly).

SILLY STATS

The world's smallest chili peppers are the Filipino Bird's Eye Chiles, which are only about two centimeters long. That's about the width of your pinkies held side by side.

206. What do you call a bear with no teeth?

A gummy bear.

207. What was wrong with the tree's car?

It wooden go.

208. Where does a peacock go when he loses his tail?

A re-tail store.

209. What do you call a sleeping stegosaurus?

A dino-snore.

210. Why did the chef wear a helmet whenever he was cooking?

Because he was on a crash diet.

211. What do clouds wear under their raincoats?

Thunderwear.

212. What do cows do for fun?

Go to the moo-vies.

213. What do you call a sad strawberry?

A blue berry.

214. Why couldn't the moon finish his meal?

He was full.

215. What else can you call a grandfather clock?

An old timer.

216. Where do salmon keep their money?

In a riverbank.

217. What do you get when you combine a vampire with a snowman?

Frost bite.

218. Where do monkeys work out?

At the jungle gym.

219. What day do Easter eggs hate?

Fry-day.

220. Why did the fraction $\frac{1}{5}$ need a massage?

Because it was two-tenths.

221. What are a squirrel's favorite flowers?

Forget-me-nuts.

222. What is an astronaut's favorite meal?

Launch.

223. What is a sheep's favorite sport?

Baa-dminton.

224. Who won the skeleton beauty pageant?

No body.

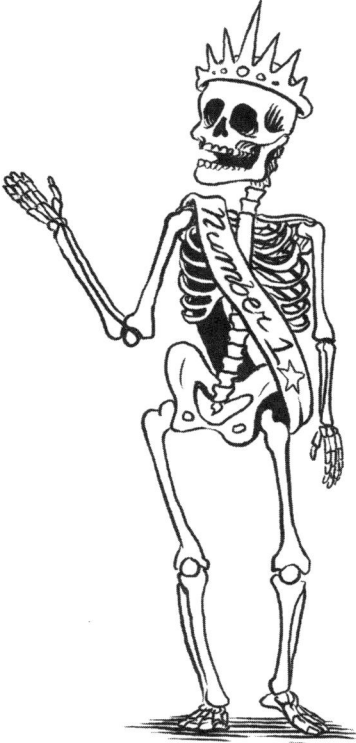

225. Why did the author install a knocker on her door?

Because she wanted to win the no-bell prize.

226. When is a door not a door?

When it's ajar.

227. What do you call two bananas?

Slippers.

228. What did the plate say to the spoon?

Dinner is on me.

229. Why did the child cross the playground?

To get to the other slide.

230. What was the wizard's favorite subject in school?

Spelling.

231. How much do pirates pay to get their ears pierced?

A buck an ear.

232. What did the parent volcano say to the baby volcano?

I lava you.

233. How do you make jellyfish laugh?

With ten tickles.

> ## SILLY STATS
>
> Jellyfish have been around for millions of years. (They were around before dinosaurs!) Some types have hundreds of tentacles.

234. How does a scientist freshen his breath?

With experi-mints.

235. How can you tell when a vampire has caught a cold?

He starts coffin.

236. Why are chemists great problem solvers?

Because they have all the solutions.

237. How does a cucumber become a pickle?

It goes through a jarring experience.

238. Why couldn't the pony sing its favorite song?

Because it was a little horse.

239. Why does the sun refuse to go to school?

Because it already has a million degrees.

240. Why did the banana go to the doctor?

Because it wasn't peeling well.

241. What do you call a funny mountain?

Hill-arious.

242. What do you call a rubber spaghetti noodle?

An impasta.

243. How do you throw a party in outer space?

You planet.

244. What do you get when you combine a centipede with a parrot?

A walkie talkie.

MIX IT UP

Practice being punny by thinking up everyday items you can rename with rhyming words. For example, your oven can make cake, in the shower you get wet, and the driveway can be car tar.

---

245. What did zero say to eight?

Nice belt.

246. What is a frog's favorite food?

French flies.

247. Why did the crouton blush?

It saw the salad dressing.

248. Why was the painting arrested?

Because it was framed.

249. Why do porcupines always win at basketball and football but never golf?

Because they always have the most points.

250. Why was the broom late?

It over-swept.

251. Why were clocks banned from the library?

Because they tock too much.

252. Where do sheep go on vacation?

The Baa-hamas.

253. What did the history book say to the math book?

You've got problems!

254. Why did the museum curator decide to become an archeologist?

Because her career was in ruins.

255. Have you heard the one about the girl who is afraid of negative numbers?

She'll stop at nothing to avoid them.

256. Name two ways to stop a bull from charging.

1) Take away its credit card.

2) Unplug its power cord.

257. Which days are the strongest?

Saturday and Sunday because the rest are week days.

258. Which letter of the alphabet holds the most water?

The C.

259. Why was Cinderella thrown off the basketball team?

Because she ran away from the ball.

260. What did one charged atom say to the other?

I've got my ion you.

261. What kind of advice can you get from your hand?

Finger tips.

262. What is a math teacher's favorite dessert?

Pi.

263. What kind of button cannot be unbuttoned?

A belly button.

264. What did the cheese say when it looked in the mirror?

Looking gouda.

265. Why did the duck stop in the middle of the road?

Because it tripped on a quack.

266. How did courageous Egyptians record their adventures?

Hero-glyphics.

RIDDLE HISTORY

Ancient Egyptians enjoyed puns, too! Many hieroglyphs included visual puns since, like English, their language had words with more than one meaning.

267. What are a pirate's least favorite vegetable?

Leeks.

268. What is the best time to go to the dentist?

Tooth-hurty.

269. Why can't you win an argument against a 90-degree angle?

Because it's always right.

270. What is a snake's favorite subject?

Hiss-tory.

271. Why was the baby strawberry crying?

Because her parents were in a jam.

272. Why is it impossible to make a reservation at the library?

Because they're always booked.

273. What do you call a cow that plays the harp?

A moo-sician.

274. What happened when oxygen went on a date with potassium?

It went OK.

275. What did the cartoonist say to his rival?

I challenge you to a doodle.

276. What kind of flower grows on your face?

Tulips.

277. Why did the thief rob the bakery?

Because there's a lot of dough.

278. Why do trees hate riddles?

Because they don't like to be stumped.

279. What do you call a dinosaur with a large vocabulary?

A thesaurus.

280. What do you call witches who share a house?

Broom-mates.

281. How do you catch a school of fish?

With a bookworm.

282. What is the strongest sea creature?

A mussel.

SILLY STATS

Mussel is the punny answer, but the real answer is the Australian Saltwater Crocodile. They can clamp their jaws shut with a force of 3,700 pounds per square inch, more than twice the strength of a hippo!

283. What did the beach say when the tide came in?

Long time, no sea.

284. What do you call a fairy that needs a bath?

Stinker bell.

285. Why can't a bicycle stand on its own?

Because it's two tired.

286. What did the townspeople call the person who only spoke in figurative language?

The Village Idiom.

287. A man is locked in a room with no windows or doors. The only items in the room are a mirror and a table. How is he able to escape? (Remember, this chapter is about puns!)

He looks in the mirror to see what he saw. He takes the saw and cuts the table in half. Next, he puts the two halves together to form a whole. Then, he simply crawls out of the room through the hole.

4

BRAIN TEASERS

(Answers begin on page 381.)

Brain teasers are puzzles that exercise your lateral thinking skills. This means you need to use creativity *and* examine the problem from multiple angles to find the answer. Technically, all the riddles in this book are brain teasers. But now that we've warmed up your creative thinking skills, we are going to tackle more challenging ones. Some might take extra time, but they're not impossible. Keep an eye out for some new tricks. At times you'll be using the information presented at face value, but other times you will need to look at the words to find patterns.

The brain teasers in this chapter will include more details. This time, you'll find the answers at the back of the book, to make it more challenging. You'll have to take all of the information into consideration and reason through it to a solution. These riddles are especially fun to work on in groups. Work together to solve them, or team up and see which team can solve the riddles fastest!

288. What word can come before the following: bag, box, and paper?

289. Mrs. Johnson baked a dozen cookies. Her 12 children came to the kitchen. Each took a cookie and left. There are 11 cookies remaining. How is this possible?

290. How is it that a typical horse can run 30 kilometers with two of its legs but 31 kilometers with the other two?

291. The 25th Amendment to the US Constitution outlines how presidential succession should be handled. If both the vice president and the Speaker of the House pass away, who becomes president?

292. Four people sat down to play together one night. They played for hours. They each had similar scores, and at the end of the evening, they each made a profit. How is it possible for all four to have made money?

293. Mr. Martinez walks into the kitchen to make breakfast. The refrigerator contains bacon, eggs, milk, and jelly. What does he open first?

294. A man works on the 42nd floor. Any time he rides the elevator alone, he goes up to the 32nd floor of his building, then walks the remaining 10 stories. When other people are in the elevator, he rides all the way up to the 42nd floor. At the end of the workday, he gets on the elevator on the 42nd floor and rides it all the way down to the lobby. He isn't taking the stairs to get exercise. Why does he get off on the 32nd floor instead of riding the elevator all the way to the 42nd floor?

295. In the town of Fibster, the townspeople always lie. In the town of Verity, the townspeople always tell the truth. It's also a law that groups of two or more must always contain at least one person from each town. At the Fibster park, you meet a boy and a girl. The boy says, "I'm Benjamin and this is my friend Imani. One of us lives in Verity." Is Benjamin telling the truth or is he fibbing?

296. How is it possible to stay underwater longer than an Olympic swimmer who can hold his breath for three minutes, without any special breathing apparatus? (Hint: It has nothing to do with technique.)

297. Which of the following numbers comes next in this series: 6, 4, 3, 11, 15, ... ?

Is it 7, 12, 17, or 20?

298. If you have seven sugar cubes that look exactly the same but have been told that one of them weighs just a little more than the others, how can you find the heavier cube by using a balance scale no more than two times?

299. A seven-letter word can be broken into two other words, and, keeping letters in the same order, be used in the following sentence: A _____ surgeon had _____ and as a result, was _____ to operate. What is the word?

300. Can you find what is unusual about this paragraph? It may look normal to you, but it is truly abnormal. As soon as you grasp it, you'll know a surprising fact. What is odd about this paragraph? Good luck! I know you can do it!

> **AROUND THE WORLD**
>
> *E* isn't just the most commonly used letter in English, it's also the most common in Dutch, Finnish, French, German, Hungarian, Italian, Norwegian, Spanish, and Swedish.

301. In a town with only two barbers, which barber should you go to for the best haircut—the one with a fantastic haircut or the one with a poor haircut?

302. A palindrome is a word or phrase that is spelled the same forward and backward. Can you think of a seven-letter palindrome that describes what you should do when a specific type of tool gets dirty?

303. Two clever siblings were trying to decide who would get the last cookie. The brother suggested that he could write the words "Yes" and "No" on two different pieces of paper. If his sister randomly chose the paper that said "Yes," she could have the last cookie. The sister worried that the brother might write "No" on both pieces of paper, making it impossible for her to select one that said "Yes." How could she succeed in getting the last cookie if her brother was already holding the pieces of paper in each hand?

304. Three kids are debating how much candy their parents have hidden. Ellie says, "Mom and Dad have at least 20 candy bars stashed away." Johnathan says, "They definitely have fewer than 20 candy bars hidden." And Katie says, "I know they are hiding at least one candy bar from us." Only one of their statements is true. Who is correct and how many candy bars do their parents have?

305. How is it possible for a car facing east to travel five miles in a straight line and end up west of where it started?

306. At the local bakery, a pie costs $6, cake costs $8, and bread costs $10. How much does a cookie cost?

307. What letter can replace the last letter of the following words: rub, bard, crows, cat?

308. According to the US Constitution, in order to become president, a candidate must be at least 35 years old, be a US citizen, have lived in the United States for at least 14 years, and be born in the United States. There is one last requirement a candidate must meet. What is it?

309. In the town of Fibster, the townspeople always lie. In the town of Verity, the townspeople always tell the truth. You meet three people at the border between the two towns and ask "Which town are you each from?" The first person whispers his response so you can't hear. The second person says, "He said he is from Verity. So am I." The third person says, "They are both from Fibster, but I'm from Verity." Which town is each of the three people from?

310. Oscar, an aspiring magician, decided on a very daring feat for his first magic trick. For his first performance, he walked across a lake without any special equipment. He succeeded in his task without getting wet, but the audience was not impressed. Why not?

311. Mason's grandfather was showing him his collection of historical memorabilia. In part of his collection, he has a newspaper dated November 11, 1918 with the headline "World War I Is Over." He also has some ancient scrolls dated 132 BCE. Mason told him that, unfortunately, those two items were worthless. Why?

312. When Mrs. Yang walked into the kitchen, she found a broken glass shattered on the floor. She immediately went to the family room to find out why whoever dropped the glass hadn't cleaned it up. As she entered the room she asked, "Who made the mess in the kitchen and didn't clean it up?" Her son Michael replied, "I haven't been in the kitchen all day." Her daughter Ava said, "It must have been Claire since she's drinking a glass of water right now!" To which Claire responded, "I didn't make the mess! The kitchen looked fine when I was in there." Who is the guilty party?

313. If you change one letter, what do the following words have in common: worth, mouth, last, best?

314. Imagine six glasses lined up in a single row. The first three are filled with water and the last three are empty. By moving only one glass, how can you arrange the glasses so that the empty and full glasses alternate? (Hint: Get creative on how and what you move.)

315. Tia tells you that she is going to the park with her father's sister's only sister-in-law's son. Who is she going to the park with?

316. There is a glass bottle sealed with a cork. Inside the bottle is a precious gemstone worth thousands of dollars. You can keep the gem if you can remove it from the bottle without breaking the glass or taking the cork out of the bottle. How do you get the gemstone out?

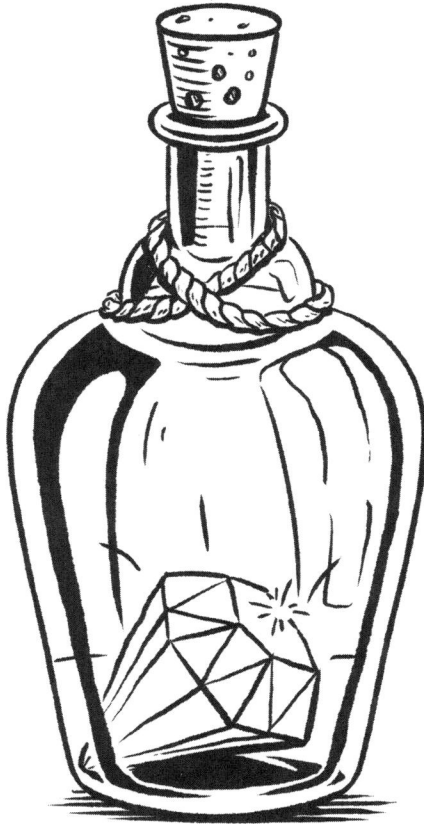

317. What four letter word can be used before the words house and sandwich and after the words book and golf?

318. The 22nd president of the United States had the same parents as the 24th president of the United States, but the 22nd and 24th president were not brothers. How is this possible? (Hint: This is fact!)

319. Yesterday, Jung walked all around town. Each time he encountered someone he would ask them a question. The question he asked was always the same. Occasionally, he would run into someone he had already encountered earlier in the day and would ask them the question again. He never received the same answer twice. What was his question?

320. What do the following words have in common: civic, madam, rotator, tenet?

321. One, Two, Three, Four, and Five are in class together. The math teacher sends Three to the principal's office for bad behavior. What was Three doing?

322. Ms. Reed has a terrible memory. She was worried she wouldn't be able to remember her computer password, which is a random assortment of letters and numbers, so she created a password hint that was foolproof. The hint is: You force heaven to be empty. What is her password?

323. If Marisa travels by car, Valerie walks, and Ivan takes the train, who rides a bicycle, Arjun or Lucas? (Hint: Look at letter patterns.)

324. What do the following words have in common: banana, dresser, grammar, potato, uneven?

325. A rich man wants to leave his inheritance to the smartest of his three children. To determine which child was wisest, he challenged them to see which son could fill the empty guest room by spending the least amount of money filling it. The first son spent $300 on a bounce house that filled the room. The second son spent $100 on 1,000 balloons to fill the room. The third son won by spending just $10. What did he buy to fill the room?

326. A group of players from the same baseball team head to the park to play a game. The final score is 7 to 7. No player touched any bases, nor did they hit any runs. How is this possible?

327. In the town of Fibster, the townspeople always lie. In the town of Verity, the townspeople always tell the truth. While getting ice cream at a truck halfway between the two cities, you want to know if the person behind you is from Fibster or Verity. To find out, you ask her to ask the person behind her in line which town he is from. You can't hear the person behind her answer, but she tells you he said he is from Verity. Is the person behind you from Fibster or Verity?

328. Which of the following sentences doesn't belong? (Hint: It's not the meaning of the sentences.)

    a)   Dev outran Greg.
    b)   Clara ate tuna.
    c)   Fred is silly.
    d)   Brianna is really driven.

329. In the town of Fibster, the townspeople always lie. In the town of Verity, the townspeople always tell the truth. On a trip to visit Verity, you come to a fork in the road, and the sign post is missing to direct you the right way. Luckily, a townsperson is there. Since you don't know which town the person is from, what can you ask him in order to know which way to go?

330. What word do the following words have in common: fall, front, melon, ski, tower?

331. What word is missing from the following sequence?

Fin, inch, chest, stew, _____, web

332. Can you find the name of a country hidden in the following sentences?

I love to sit outside to enjoy the sun and the wind. I am an outdoor person for sure!

333. Zara was traveling to the local farmers' market along Main Street. On the way there, she met a family with eight children. Each child held two bags. Each bag held three fish. How many people were traveling to the farmers' market?

RIDDLE HISTORY

This riddle was inspired by the "As I was going to St. Ives" riddle, which was found in a book written in 1730. The original riddle is: "As I was going to St. Ives, I met a man with seven wives. Each wife had seven sacks, each sack had seven cats, each cat had seven kits: kits, cats, sacks, and wives, how many were going to St. Ives?" (The answer there is one as well!)

---

334. Hiroshi is having a birthday party and his mother has already sliced the cake into eight slices. Just before the cake is served, the neighbors swing by and now the party has doubled in size. Hiroshi's mother manages to slice the cake into 16 pieces by making only *one* more cut. How does she manage this?

BRAIN BENDER

335. There are three switches by the front door that control three different light bulbs in the basement. How can you figure out which light switch controls each light bulb if you can only make one trip to the basement?

5

FUN WITH MATH

(Answers begin on page 387.)

Math is a great way to practice problem solving and critical thinking. It takes logic, looking for patterns, and methodically working through each step. When armed with strong math skills, we can create order from chaos. It's how construction workers turn a pile of wood into a home, or how a chef turns a bag of groceries into a gourmet meal.

The riddles in this chapter are going to help you flex your math muscles. There are no trick questions, and once again you'll find the answers at the back of the book. You should be able to solve each riddle by using basic math. The only challenge is figuring out which of your math skills to use for each problem. Grab a pencil and paper. They'll help you work out some of the more challenging riddles ahead. Some hints are offered, but try to use them only if you're stumped.

336. 20 + 20 + 20 = 60.

How can you get to the sum of 60 with three identical digits that *aren't* 20?

337. What is the three-digit number where the following are true: the first digit is one more than the last, the second is greater than the first and last, and the sum of all three digits is 16? Start by experimenting with different numbers, placing them where they might fit the description.

338. How many times does the digit 8 occur between 0 and 100? (Hint: This is trickier than you think!)

339. All the digits from 1 to 9 are used in the equation below. Can you fill in the blanks? (Hint: Start with information you know must be true. What combinations are possible to get the given answer so far? Once you figure out the first number, go from there.)

___ 6 ___ + 3 ___ 7 = ___ 1 ___

340. What number is missing in the following sequence? (Hint: Think creatively, not necessarily mathematically.)

16, 06, 68, 88, ___, 98

341. If four painters can paint four rooms in two days, how long will it take one painter to paint six rooms?

342. If you walk to your friend's house at five miles per hour, discover he's not home, and return home walking at three miles per hour, how far away does your friend live if the total trip took you 48 minutes? (Hint: Your pace on the way to your friend's house was 12 minutes per mile, and on the way back it was 20 minutes per mile.)

343. Sebastian brought some snacks to share with Zain and Randall. The snacks were divided equally between all three friends. Each of the friends ate half of their snacks. Then, Zain ate one-fourth of his remaining snacks. Sebastian ate three-fourths of his remaining snacks, leaving him with just two. Randall ate one-eighth of his remaining snacks. How many snacks did they start with? (Hint: Look at the second sentence. The number must be equally divided by three, and large enough for there to be leftovers.)

344. Sofia has two more sisters than she has brothers. Her brother Val has three times as many sisters as brothers. There are fewer than 10 children in the family. How many are girls and how many are boys? (Hint: You can experiment by starting at nine [fewer than 10 children] and going backward, or starting at one brother and multiplying by two until you get to an even number under 10.)

345. Miguel is 12 years old. Mia is half Miguel's age. How old will Mia be when Miguel is 100?

346. Three hot dogs and four bottles of water cost $10. Two hot dogs and two bottles of water cost $6. What is the price of each hot dog and each bottle of water? Try experimenting with different prices.

347. Marion is four times the age that Jamie was three years ago. In two more years, Marion will be double Jamie's current age. Added together, their ages today equal 13. How old is each of them? (Hint: Start with what you know, which is their total current age, and work from there. What age splits are possible today? What are their current minimum ages?)

348. In the problems below, each letter stands for a different digit. If T = 8, can you figure out the value of the rest of the letters?

CAT + DOG = PET

PAN + DOG = TEN

MIX IT UP

See if you can make another equation with real words using the same letter assignments from this riddle. You don't have to stick with three-letter words or addition.

---

349. Adrien and Amari decide to bet on coin tosses. Each time the coin lands on heads, Amari must pay Adrien $1. If the coin lands on tails, Adrien must pay Amari $1. When they are done, Adrien has won three times, but Amari ends with $5. How many times did they flip the coin?

350. By looking at the pattern below, can you figure out which number comes next?

2, 3, 5, 8, 12, ?

MIX IT UP

Make a contest out of solving sequences by racing a friend or family member to see who can find the answer fastest!

---

351. Place +, -, ×, and ÷ in between the numbers below to make an equation that is correct. Solve the equation left to right (ignore typical mathematical order of operations). All four symbols must be used once.

2 __ 9 __ 3 __ 1 __ 4 = 8

MIX IT UP

We ignore the order of operations for this problem to make it easier to solve. This wouldn't be correct on a math test! Remember to always multiply and divide before you add and subtract.

---

352. If Wyatt buys a baseball card for $5 and sells it to Rory for $7, but later buys it back for $10, only to sell it again for $12, how much profit does he make, if any?

353. A music teacher needs to order recorders for his students. Knowing he would need over 100, when the math teacher asked how many he was ordering, the music teacher decided to have some fun with his reply. He said:

- If I order in twos, I'll be short one recorder.
- If I order in groups of three, I'll be short two recorders.
- If I order in groups of four, I'll be short three recorders.
- If I order in groups of five, I'll be short four recorders.
- If I order in groups of six, I'll be short five recorders.
- I must order in groups of seven to obtain just the right amount.

How many recorders will he order?

354. Imagine you have a box in front of you filled with $1, $5, $10, and $20 bills. You are allowed to take one bill at a time from the box until you have taken four bills of the same value (e.g., four $10 bills). What is the most money you can possibly draw before accomplishing this?

355. What is the four-digit number where the following are true: the first digit is double the second, the third is half of the fourth, the second is less than the third, and the sum of the digits is 15?

356. If a tree doubles in height every year until it reaches its maximum height at 10 years, how many years does it take for the tree to reach half of its maximum height? (Hint: It's not five years.)

SILLY STATS

The Empress tree is the fastest growing hardwood tree in the world. It grows up to 20 feet its first year and can reach a height of up to 50 feet!

---

357. Mrs. Wilson washed a bunch of cherries and set them in a large bowl for her three children to snack on. When Alex noticed them on the counter, he ate one-third to leave equal portions for his brother and sister. Later, Alyssa discovered the cherries and, not realizing Alex had already eaten some, only ate one-third to leave enough for her brothers. When Tyler saw the cherries, he also only ate one-third to be sure to save some for his siblings. If there were eight cherries left after Tyler had eaten his share, how many cherries were in the bowl at the beginning? (Hint: Remember eight is one-third of what Tyler started with before he ate his share.)

358. What two digits create a one-digit answer if they are multiplied together but a two-digit answer if they are added together?

359. Notice 2 + 2 = 4 and 2 × 2 = 4. Find three whole numbers, each a different digit, that equal the same number whether they're added together or multiplied.

360. When Mr. Malik slammed on his brakes to avoid hitting a mother goose crossing the road with her six goslings, it caused a 10-car bumper-to-bumper pile-up accident behind him. How many bumpers were damaged in the accident?

361. What is ½ of ⅔ of ¾ of ⅘ of ⅚ of 6/7 of ⅞ of 8/9 of 9/10 of 1000? (Hint: Start at the end.)

362. Mateo, Samia, and Nikki are hungry and craving hamburgers for lunch. Unfortunately, their grill can only fit two hamburger patties at one time. Since each side takes five minutes to cook, it will be 20 minutes before all three hamburgers are done. Mateo realizes there's a way to completely cook all three burgers in just 15 minutes. Can you figure out how?

363. Ms. Brown has a grandfather clock that chimes every hour on the hour and at every half hour. On the half hour, it always chimes once. At each hour, it chimes according to the time (i.e., one chime at one o'clock, two chimes at two o'clock, three chimes at three o'clock, etc.). If Ms. Brown arrives home and hears a chime as she enters, another chime 30 minutes later, and one chime after another 30 minutes, what time did Ms. Brown arrive home?

RIDDLE HISTORY

Grandfather clocks are named after a song written in 1875 by an American songwriter. He wrote the song "My Grandfather's Clock" about a clock at an inn he'd visited that stopped working at the exact time the inn's owner passed away.

364. When you add Harper's age to her mother's, the sum is 55. Harper's age is the reverse of her mother's. How old is Harper and how hold is her mother? (Note: Harper is a teenager.)

365. Carter loves animals. All his pets are dogs except two. Oddly, all his pets are cats except two. Stranger yet, all his pets are birds except two. How many pets does Carter have?

366. There are 20 socks in a laundry basket. Ten of the socks are white and 10 of the socks are gray. If you were blindfolded, what is the fewest number of socks you could pick from the basket to be certain you were holding a matching pair?

367. If we know a pencil costs $1 more than an eraser, and that together they cost $1.20, can you figure out how much an eraser costs purchased separately? (Hint: It's not 20 cents!)

368. In the puzzle below, each letter stands for a different digit. If F = 9, can you figure out which numbers each of the other letters represents?

FUN – ONE = HON

BUT – NO = BOW

369. If it takes one child 30 seconds to sharpen a pencil, how long does it take three children to sharpen 12 pencils, assuming each child has their own pencil sharpener?

370. Kai and Carmen go to the beach to collect shark teeth. They agree to split the shark teeth evenly at the end of the day so each has the same number. When they are done, they realize that if Kai gives Carmen one tooth, Carmen will have twice as many as Kai. However, if Carmen gives Kai one tooth, they'll have an equal number. How many shark teeth did each person collect?

371. Kabir is trying to climb a hill that is 150 feet tall. Unfortunately, the hill is very muddy, so for every three feet Kabir travels forward, he slides back one foot. How many feet total will Kabir have walked by the time he reaches the top of the hill?

372. Mrs. Palmer likes to boil her tea for exactly seven minutes. Being rather old-fashioned, she doesn't have a regular kitchen timer, but instead uses hourglass timers. She has a 3-minute timer, a 5-minute timer, and a 10-minute timer. How can she use her available timers to make sure she boils her tea for exactly seven minutes?

373. What number comes next in the series?

1, 3, 6, 10, 15, 21, ?

374. Aaron has 100 pennies. He distributes the coins into four different bags. Each bag has two more pennies than the bag filled before it. How many pennies are in each bag?

375. In front of you are three bags, each containing two marbles. You know that one bag contains two white marbles, one bag contains two black marbles, and that the third bag contains one white marble and one black marble, but you don't know which bag contains which marbles. If you pick a bag at random and remove a white marble, is it more likely or less likely that the other marble in the bag is white?

376. A fox is 10 yards away from a rabbit when it begins chasing it. The rabbit is 40 yards away from its hole. The fox can run 5 yards per second, but the rabbit can only run 4 yards per second. Will the rabbit make it to its hole before the fox catches it?

MIX IT UP

Another way to solve this problem would be to make a graph that shows the rabbit's and fox's starting locations and mark their progress after each second.

---

377. The digits 1, 2, and 3 have been randomly assigned to the letters A, B, and C. Using the clues below, can you determine which letters symbolize which digits?

BCBA is smaller than ABAB, which is smaller than CABC. The sum of the digits in the largest number is 9.

378. Aubrey is building a house of cards using eight decks of cards (a total of 416 cards). On the first day, she places 162 cards. To avoid making it collapse, each day she places only two-thirds of the number of cards as the day before. How many days will it take to complete her house of cards?

379. What is the four-digit number where the following are true: the second digit is double the third, the first is greater than the last, the last is the smallest, and the sum of the digits is 15?

380. Place +, -, ×, and ÷ in between the numbers below to make an equation that is correct. Solve the equation left to right (ignore the typical mathematical order of operations). All four symbols must be used once.

4 _ 3 _ 6 _ 8 _ 1 = 9

381. Omar and Kam go to buy school supplies and agree to share the items and the expense. Omar buys a package of pencil grips for $1. Kam buys some stickers for $2 and a pack of markers for $4. How much does Omar owe Kam?

382. Can you figure out the pattern in the following sequence sets to determine the missing number?

4, 3, 2	10, 6, 8	15, 7, 16
7, 5, 4	8, 1, 14	12, 3, ?

⬤ **BRAIN BENDER** ⬤

383. Theo's parents decide to give him an allowance. It will start out at $5 per month but will increase by $1 every month. Emery's parents also decide to start paying a similar allowance but decide to pay her twice a month. So, Emery's allowance starts at $2.50 and will increase by 25 cents every time she gets paid. Who will make more money in the first three months? Who will make more money at the end of one year?

6

LOGIC PUZZLES

(Answers begin on page 394.)

I've saved my very favorite type of riddles for last: logic puzzles! To solve the riddles in this chapter, you're going to use deductive reasoning to eliminate options until you reach the correct solution. You will have to pay close attention to details in order to solve these puzzles. And again, you'll find the answers at the back of the book.

Like the math challenges in the preceding chapter, these puzzles aren't meant to trick you. They're intended to exercise your deductive reasoning. You should give yourself a pat on the back for each logic puzzle you complete. The skills required to solve them are hard to master, but they will benefit you for the rest of your life!

384. Can you think of a four-letter word that describes a way you communicate and that, when you change the third letter, becomes something you must do?

385. Five friends each have a different favorite class at school. Can you use the clues below to figure out which class is each friend's favorite?

- Neither Samir nor Kendall like science, and Samir also dislikes reading.

- Harley's favorite subject is music.

- Eden's favorite subject is either math or science.

- Drew enjoys social studies the most.

386. There is one letter that, if added to each of the following four-letter words, will form three new five-letter words. What is the letter?

    CHAT   BLOW   REST

387. Complete the following analogy: Scarf is to neck as ring is to _____.

    Is the correct answer hand, finger, glove, or phone?

388. Paris, Raven, and Corey are friends. One friend plays soccer, another plays baseball, and one plays basketball. Use the clues below to figure out who plays which sport.

- The baseball player doesn't have any siblings and doesn't own a bicycle.

- Paris rides her bicycle to soccer practice with Corey's brother.

RIDDLE HISTORY

This riddle is the most common type of logic puzzle. They often include grids where you can eliminate options based on the clues to narrow in on the solution. Try using grids for the puzzles in this book!

---

389. Mr. Williams lives about an hour from the closest town, so he only goes into town once a week. When he goes to town, he goes to the bank to withdraw cash for shopping, the market to pick up vegetables, the butcher to get meat, and the bakery for fresh bread. The bank is open Monday through Friday. The market is closed on Thursday or Friday. The butcher is open on Tuesday, Thursday, and Saturday. And the bakery is open every day except Wednesday. What day does Mr. Williams go to town to run his errands?

390. Five children decided to race across the park. Lulu finished before Dani, but after Mila. Owen got to the finish line before Elijah, but after Dani. What order did the children finish in?

391. There are four houses of four different colors (red, blue, yellow, and green). In each house lives a person from a different country (England, Japan, Kenya, and Mexico). Each homeowner has a different pet (dog, cat, bird, and fish). Using the following clues, can you tell who owns the fish?

- The person from England lives in the red house.

- The person from Mexico has a cat.

- The owner of the green house has a dog.

- Neither the Japanese person nor the Kenyan owns a bird.

- The owner of the blue house is not from Mexico or Japan.

RIDDLE HISTORY

Rumor has it that a riddle very similar to this was created by Albert Einstein (the original riddle has five houses, five people, five pets, and a couple of other unique characteristics). Other people say the original riddle was written by Lewis Carroll, the author of *Alice's Adventures in Wonderland*.

---

392. A farmer is traveling with his dog, a rabbit, and some lettuce he is delivering to a friend. He reaches a river that he will have to cross, but the boat on the riverbank will only fit him and one other item. He cannot leave the dog alone with the rabbit, nor can he leave the rabbit alone with the lettuce. How can he transport all three across the river safely in the boat? (Hint: He makes more than one trip.)

RIDDLE HISTORY

River-crossing riddles have been traced back to the year 735 when a scholar wrote a book that included these riddles, titled *Propositiones ad Acuendos Juvenes* (which means "Problems to Sharpen the Young").

393. In Min-seo's class, 12 students had red in their shirts, 10 students had blue in their shirts, and 6 students had yellow in their shirts. Of those students, 8 had both red and blue in their shirts, 3 had red and yellow, and 1 had red, blue, and yellow in their shirt. How many students were wearing solid colored shirts? How many of the solid colored shirts were red? How many were blue? How many were yellow?

394. Jules has a bowl of chocolate-covered candies. The following statements about it are true:

- All the candies with peanuts inside are red.
- Jules likes all the candies in the bowl.
- Jules does not like red candies.

Are there any candies with peanuts in the bowl?

395. Find words that rhyme with each of the words below. The first word is a category. The three words after that are words that fit within that category.

- The name of the category rhymes with SLUMBER.
- The words in the category rhyme with GATE, SIGN, and HEN.

What are the words?

396. Mr. and Mrs. Smith have three daughters and one son. Each of their children has a different favorite color: red, blue, green, or yellow. Likewise, each child has a unique favorite fruit: bananas, cherries, kiwi, or oranges. Can you figure out which child has which preferences based on the facts below?

- Their daughter Joyce likes blue and doesn't like bananas or kiwi.

- Another daughter, Ruby, likes a color that is made by combining her brother's favorite color with one of her sister's favorite colors.

- Camilla's favorite fruit's color is also her favorite color, unlike Isaac's favorite fruit and color.

397. Can you think of a five-letter word that represents a mode of transportation, which, when you change the last letter, becomes something that grows in dirt?

398. Complete the following analogy: Acorn is to forest as seed is to _____.

Is the correct answer fruit, tree, orchard, or plant?

399. There is one letter that, if added to each of the following four-letter words, will form three new five-letter words. What is the letter? (Hint: The letter doesn't have to go in the same place.)

RUBY   THIN   SURE

400. The word DAYBREAK is interesting because not only can it be broken into two words by separating DAY from BREAK, but you can also form two new words by separating its odd and even letters. If you take each of its odd letters (DYRA), you can rearrange them into a new word. Likewise, if you take all its even letters, you can rearrange them to make a different word. What are the two words?

RIDDLE HISTORY

When words like "daybreak" can be broken down into anagrams for two different words by taking their alternating letters, they are referred to as *alterposal*.

401. Four explorers decide to explore a cave. Just as they reach a bridge that leads to the cave, their flashlight batteries die. Thankfully, one of the explorers has a backup flashlight, though it will only work for 15 minutes. Only two people can be on the bridge at one time. Each of the explorers walks at a different pace. Chloe can cross the bridge in just one minute, but it takes Amit two minutes to cross. Maliah needs five minutes to cross and Oliver needs a full eight minutes to get across the bridge. If two people walk across together, they will travel at the slower person's speed. How can they all get across the bridge in 15 minutes before the flashlight goes out? (Yes, it's possible! Hint: The fastest explorers will cross first and last.)

402. Complete the following analogy: Hungry is to food as dry is to _____.

Is the correct answer wet, desert, hot, or moisture?

403. When cleaning up his classroom, Mr. Jackson accidentally sorted his pencils and erasers into bins with the wrong labels. One bin is labeled "PENCILS," another bin is labeled "ERASERS," and the third bin is labeled "PENCILS & ERASERS." None of the bins have been sorted correctly, so each of the three bins bears the wrong label. Without looking in the bins, how could you correct the labels by removing only one item from one bin?

404. A family of four (two parents and two children) is on a backpacking trip, and they reach a river. A kind fisherman offers to let the family use his small boat to make the crossing. Unfortunately, the boat is only large enough to hold one adult or two children. How can the family use the boat to make the crossing and return the boat to the fisherman? (Hint: There are more than 10 trips across the water!)

AROUND THE WORLD

This riddle is similar to one that is supposedly an IQ test given to job applicants for certain jobs in Japan. In that version there is also a thief and a policeman, adding even more complexity to the puzzle!

---

405. By changing one letter in each of the words below, you can turn the words into two new words that are antonyms of each other. What are the two words you can create?

KEEP   SWALLOW

406. Can you think of a four-letter word that describes a mild temperature, which, when you change the first letter, becomes a place people like to visit in the summer?

407. Can you change the word WARM to COLD in four steps by only changing one letter in the word at a time so that each change creates a real word? (There will be a total of three words in between.) It's called a word ladder. (Hint: The first letter change is a consonant.)

408. The word INTEREST is interesting because if you take each of its odd letters, you can rearrange them into a new word. Likewise, if you take all its even letters, you can rearrange them to make a different word. What are the two words?

409. Complete the following analogy: Pencil is to write as broom is to _____.

Is the correct answer mop, dustpan, sweep, or dirt?

410. Dominique, Aidan, Yuki, and Zara all have birthdays this month. They will be turning 5, 8, 10, and 12, but not in that order. For their gifts, one of them is getting a puppy, one is getting a bike, one is getting a video game, and one is getting clothes. Can you figure out how old each person is turning and what they are getting for their birthday using the clues below?

- The 10-year-old is getting the bike.

- Dominique, who is the youngest, is not getting a puppy.

- The clothes are going to the oldest person, who is not Aidan.

- Yuki, who is not the oldest, is getting a puppy.

411. Find words that rhyme with each of the words below. The first word is a category. The three words after that are words that fit within that category.

- The name of the category rhymes with PINK.

- The words in the category rhyme with SILK, DAUGH-TER, and TRUCE.

What are the words?

412. The word DISLOYAL is interesting because you can take each of its odd letters and rearrange them into a new word. Likewise, you can take all its even letters and rearrange them to make a different word. What are the two words?

413. Violet, Magenta, and Rose showed up at a party in new dresses. Violet said, "Isn't it funny that we are wearing dresses that match our names, but none of us is wearing a dress that matches our own name?" The girl in the rose-colored dress looked around and said, "That is funny!" What color was each girl wearing?

414. There is one letter that, if added to each of the following four-letter words, will form three new five-letter words. What is the letter?

TANK   ACES   LATER

415. Complete the following analogy: Sister is to sibling as father is to _____.

Is the correct answer parent, mother, uncle, or brother?

416. At summer camp, three of the boys and three of the girls are challenged to find a way to get their group across the river in a two-person boat with the following condition: There can never be more boys than girls together. How can they get everyone across without violating the condition? Remember, the boat has to return with someone in it each time. (Hint: There are six round trips.)

417. By changing one letter in each of the words below, you can turn the words into two new words that are antonyms of each other. What are the two words you can create?

    LEADER   FOSTER

418. Can you change the word HEAD to TOES in five steps by only changing one letter in the word at a time? Each change must create a real word. Since there is more than one way to solve it, make the ladder so the first change/step is something you're doing right now, and the third step is a small amphibian that lives in ponds. There will be four words in between HEAD and TOES in this word ladder.

419. Can you think of a five-letter common Halloween costume which, when you remove a letter, becomes someone in charge of a party?

420. Luciana, Langston, Levi, Lincoln, and Lillian play on separate soccer teams. Their team names are the Bobcats, the Eagles, the Firebirds, the Pythons, and the Raptors. Each team has a different color jersey: blue, orange, yellow, purple, and red. Can you use the clues below to figure out what team each person is on and which color jersey they wear?

- Both Luciana's and Lincoln's jersey colors start with the same letter as their team names.

- Langston does not play for the Firebirds or the Pythons, but Lillian does.

- Levi plays for the Eagles and wears an orange jersey.

- Lincoln's jersey is the color combination of Luciana's and Lillian's jerseys.

- Levi's jersey is the color combination of Langston's and Lillian's jerseys.

421. Find words that rhyme with each of the words below. The first word is a category. The three words after that are words that fit within that category.

- The name of the category rhymes with FENCES.
- The words in the category rhyme with MUCH, KITE, and FELL.

What are the words?

422. Complete the following analogy: Breeze is to tornado as trickle is to _____.

Is the correct answer rain, earthquake, wind, or tidal wave?

423. If you change one letter in each of the words below, you can turn them into synonyms of one another. What are the three words? (Hint: It's not the same letter in each.)

START   CLOVER   BRAWNY

424. By changing one letter in each of the words below, you can turn the words into two new words that are antonyms of each other. What are the two words you can create?

PALS   MAIL

425. In one city, there are five different food trucks (tacos, pizza, gyros, salads, and hot dogs) on five different streets (Apple Ave., Badger Blvd., Charles Ct., Dominican Dr., and River Rd.). The five owners of the different food trucks are Ariel, Bailey, Cameron, Devon, and Riley. Each food truck serves a different number of items (4, 5, 6, 7, or 8). Using the clues below, can you figure out who owns which truck, where it is parked, and how many items they sell?

- Only the hot dog truck is parked on a street that starts with the same letter as its owner's name.

- Ariel does not sell tacos, hot dogs, or salads, but she does sell more items than anyone else besides Devon.

- Bailey sells gyros and sells fewer items than Cameron.

- The taco truck on Badger Blvd. is not owned by Devon.

- The salad truck sells the widest variety of items.

- The truck on Dominican Dr. does not sell gyros or hot dogs.

- The truck on River Rd. sells either gyros or salads and has fewer items than the hot dog truck.

- The pizza truck does not belong to Riley, who sells more items than Cameron but fewer than Devon.

7

YOUR TURN!

Congratulations on mastering all kinds of riddles! Are you ready to write some of your own? Coming up with riddles is just as much fun as solving them! If you have a friend or family member who enjoys riddles, too, make up riddles to try to stump each other. That way, you can create *and* solve riddles—the best of both worlds! It can be a little intimidating to come up with riddles from scratch, which is why I'm going to give you some guidelines and templates to make it easy to get started.

Write Your Own Riddles

Look for common objects in your home and make a list of each one's features. Choose some of those features that may have dual meanings or that are descriptive but won't give away the item too quickly.

> **Example:** Consider a pillow. It's white, soft, and fluffy. It's where you rest your head at night. It can be used as a weapon (*in a pillow fight*). It lives inside a case (*a pillowcase*).

Now think about something you enjoy and choose something about it to be your answer. Then brainstorm interesting ways to describe it that might stump someone.

> **Example:** If you like reading, your answer might be a bookmark. One tricky way to describe it would be to say that without it, you might lose track of where you are and have trouble finishing an adventure.

Practice being punny. Choose a topic and think of silly puns that fit it. Then, create a riddle that would lead someone to the punny solution.

> **Example:** Let's choose baked goods for our topic. Some puns related to it are: donut (*do not*) let me down, I had a filling (*feeling*) you would say that, and I whisk (*wish*) you wouldn't.

For an easy math riddle, write down a three-digit number. Then, make up clues that accurately describe the digits' relationships to one another.

> **Example:** Let's say we choose the number 471. We can say that the sum of the digits is 12, the first digit is even, the last digit is the smallest, and the middle digit is the greatest.

Sometimes there is more than one right answer to these kinds of riddles, so be prepared if someone comes up with an acceptably correct (or not wrong!) response. It might end up being pretty funny!

For logic puzzles, start with the names of three people. Then, select some characteristics they will each vary on. Decide which person will have which characteristics and construct clues that share enough details for someone to solve the riddle, without giving too much away. With these types of riddles, always be certain to try to solve your riddle using the clues you've provided to be sure you've included enough information to make the problem solvable.

> **Example:** Let's start with Aisha, Brian, and Kat. Each of them plays a different instrument and prefers a different style of music. We'll need to make sure to list all the instruments and musical styles and provide enough clues to cover all those options.

Create Your Own Clever Q&A Riddles

What has [*word that has two meanings*] but cannot [*verb that goes with the most common understanding of the feature*]?

Example: What has [*legs*] but cannot [*walk*]?

A table.

Create Your Own "What Am I?" Riddles

I am [*adjective*] and [*another adjective*]. People like [*feature that makes item likeable*]. You will not find me [*place you'd never find item*], but you may find me [*place you'd most likely find item*]. What am I?

Example: I am round and flat. People like to have me for breakfast. You will not find me in the oven, but you might find me on the stove.

(Answer: A pancake)

Create Your Own Puns

What did the [*noun*] say to the [*another noun*]?

Example: What did the window say to the mirror?

(Answer: "Hey, good looking.")

Create Your Own Brain Teasers

What do the following words have in common? [*List words you've chosen with something in common.*]

> **Example:** What do the following words have in common? Ball, thing, bummer, splinter. (*They rhyme with the four seasons: fall, spring, summer, winter.*)

Create Your Own Fun Math Riddles

By looking at the pattern below, can you determine which number comes next? [*Come up with a rule and generate numbers that fit it.*]

> **Example:** 1, 2, 4, 8, 16, ?
>
> > (Answer: 32. Each number doubles the preceding number.)

Create Your Own Logic Analogies

Complete the following analogy: [*adjective that describes noun*] is to [*noun described by adjective*] as [*adjective*] is to_____.

> **Example:** Red is to apple as yellow is to (*banana*).

Answer Key

Chapter 4: Brain Teasers

288. Sand.

289. "Each" is the name of one of her children. Only the child named Each took a cookie.

290. It can happen when the horse is running around a track! The legs closer to the outside of the track travel farther than the legs on the inner side of the track.

291. The president remains the president.

292. The four people are musicians who were hired to perform at an event.

293. The refrigerator door.

294. He's too short to reach the buttons for the higher floors.

295. Benjamin is telling the truth. Since we know that one of them must be from Fibster and the other one must be from Verity, Benjamin's statement is accurate.

296. Fill a cup or bowl with water and stand under it for longer than three minutes. Technically, you'll have stayed "underwater" for longer.

297. It's 17. Each number in the series has one more letter when spelled out than the previous number. Since 15 has eight letters, the next number must have nine letters: S-E-V-E-N-T-E-E-N.

298. First, place three sugar cubes on each side of the scale. If the scale balances, the seventh cube that wasn't weighed is the heavier one, and you don't need a second weighing. If one side is heavier than the other, set the three from the lighter side aside. For the second time using the scale, place one cube from the heavier side on one side of the scale, and a second cube on the other side of the scale. If the scale balances, the third cube from the original heavy side is the heavy cube. If the scale doesn't balance, the heavier cube will be alone on the heavy side.

299. NOTABLE: notable, no table, not able

300. The letter e doesn't appear in it, which is unusual since e is the most commonly used letter in the English language.

301. You should go to the one with the poor haircut, since they are the only other barber in town and must have given the fantastic haircut.

302. Wash saw.

303. If the sister is correct that her brother wrote "No" on both pieces, she should tear up the piece of paper she chooses without looking at it. They will then have to look at the other piece of paper she *didn't* choose. If it says "No," that means the torn-up pieces *should* have said "Yes." She will not only get the cookie, but outsmart her sneaky brother.

304. Johnathan is right and the parents aren't hiding any candy. If Katie's statement is correct then all statements are true, and only one statement is right. If Ellie's statement is correct, so is Katie's, which is impossible, as we know only one statement can be correct. Since Katie's statement cannot be correct, then Jonathan is right and the parents must be hiding *less* than one candy bar, which is zero.

305. By driving in reverse.

306. A cookie is $12. The bakery charges $2 per letter in the baked good's name.

307. Each of them can be turned into a new word by replacing the last letter of the word with the letter *n*.

308. They must be elected.

309. The first two people are from Verity and the third is from Fibster. Since people from Fibster always lie and people from Verity always tell the truth, when asked where they are from, both will always say they are from Verity. Thus, even though you didn't hear the first person's response, we know he must have said he was from Verity, so the second person was telling the truth.

310. The lake was frozen, so it was easy to walk across.

311. They are fake. No one referred to World War I by that name until World War II began. Since BCE and CE weren't used until the year 1582, it would be impossible to find authentic scrolls dated correctly before then (especially when no one prior to year 0 would know what they were counting down to!). Therefore, the items are worthless.

312. It's Ava. If the other two were telling the truth, the mess must have happened after Claire was in the kitchen, and Michael hadn't been in there all day. But the real clue is that Mrs. Yang didn't mention that the mess was a broken glass. Only the person who broke the glass would know what the mess was.

313. If you change the first letter of each word, you can turn them into directions: north, south, east, and west.

314. Pick up the second glass and pour the water into the fifth glass and return the now-empty glass to its original position.

315. Her brother.

316. Push the cork into the bottle and pour the gemstone out.

317. Club.

318. They were the same person: Grover Cleveland.

319. What time is it?

320. They are all palindromes (spelled the same backward and forward).

321. Being "mean."

322. U472BMT. You=U, force heaven = 47, to = 2, be = B, empty = MT.

323. Lucas. Each person's mode of transportation shares the same third letter with the person's name.

324. If you take away the first letter, the remaining letters are the same forward and backward.

325. He bought a candle and matches. He lit the candle and filled the room with light.

326. They were playing soccer, not baseball.

327. She is from Verity. No matter where the person behind her was from, he would have answered "Verity" (if he was from Verity, he'd tell the truth and say Verity, and if he was from Fibster, he'd lie and say Verity). If she was from Verity, she'd tell the truth and say that he said he was from Verity. If she was from Fibster, she'd lie and say he was from Fibster. Since we know his answer had to be Verity, that means she told the truth, which means she is from Verity.

328. C. "Fred is silly." The first letter of the word in each sentence spells out an animal (A = dog, B = cat, D = bird).

329. Ask him which path leads to his village. If he is from Verity, he will point you toward Verity since he will tell the truth. If he is from Fibster, he will also point you toward Verity since he will be dishonest.

330. All of them can be preceded by the word "water."

331. Ewe. Each word in the sequence begins with the last two letters of the word before it.

332. India (starting after the "w" in wind and ending before the "m" in am).

333. One. Just Zara, who was on her way to the market. Since the family members she met were carrying bags of food, they were walking the opposite direction on Main Street.

334. She slices the cake in half separating top from bottom.

BRAIN BENDER

335. Turn on the first two switches and leave them on for several minutes. Then, turn the first switch off. Go to the basement. The light that is on is the one that is controlled by the second switch. Feel the two bulbs that are off. The one that is warm is controlled by the first switch. (It will be warm from being on for several minutes before you turned it off.)

Chapter 5: Fun with Math

336. 55 + 5 = 60 (Tricky, right? Never said it had to be a set of three identical numbers!)

337. 574.

338. Nineteen: 8, 18, 28, 38, 48, 58, 68, 78, 80, 81, 82, 83, 84, 85, 86, 87, 88, 89, 98.

339. 462 + 357 = 819

340. 87. The numbers are upside down. If you turn them right side up, you'll see they count up from 86 to 91.

341. 12 days. It takes each painter two days to paint one room. Two days times six rooms equals 12 days total.

342. 1.5 miles. To solve this puzzle, use the formula $12x + 20x = 48$ (12 minutes/mile times the distance to your friend's house plus 20 minutes/mile times the return distance in 48 total minutes.)

343. 48. If Sebastian's two snacks were one-fourth of what he had left, that means he must have had eight snacks. But before he ate those eight, remember they each ate half of the original snacks Sebastian brought. That means he would have had started with 16. Sixteen snacks times three friends is 48 total snacks. Verify the math this way: If each were given 16, each ate 8 at the start, leaving them with 8 each. Zain then ate one-fourth of his 8, or 2. Randall ate one-eighth of his, or 1. Sebastian ate three-fourths of his 8, or 6 (leaving two).

344. Six girls and three boys.

345. Mia will be 94 since she is six years younger than Miguel. (Many people think this is easy and answer too quickly, without thinking; many guess the answer is 50, incorrectly thinking she will still be half his age.)

346. Hot dogs are $2 each. Each water bottle costs $1.

347. Marion is 8 and Jamie is 5.

348. A = 1, C = 2, D = 3, E = 7, G = 0, N = 4, O = 6, P = 5, T = 8

349. Eleven. Adrien lost three times to Amari, so Adrien had lost $3 at some point in the game. Adrien would have to have won another three games to win back those $3, plus another five games to end up with $5 at the end.

350. 17. Each increase is one more than the one before (add one to the first number, add two to the second, three to the third ...), so the fifth number will have five added to it, and the next number will be five more than 12: $1 + 2 = 3, 2 + 3 = 5, 3 + 5 = 8, 4 + 8 = 12, 5 + 12 = 17$.

351. $2 + 9 \times 3 - 1 \div 4 = 8$

352. He makes a profit of $4. He's initially out $5, so $-$5 + $7 = $2 profit. Then he pays 10 new dollars and sells for $12, earning a new $2 profit. $2 + $2 = $4.

353. 119.

354. $128. You could draw three of each denomination and finally draw a fourth $20 bill. $3 \times 1 + 3 \times 5 + 3 \times 10 + 4 \times 20 = \$128$.

355. 4,236.

356. Nine years. Since it doubles in size every year, the year before it reaches its maximum height, it will be at half its maximum height.

357. 27. The eight that were left were two-thirds of what Alyssa left, so she must have left 12. Twelve was two-thirds of what Alex had left, meaning Tyler started with 18. Eighteen was two-thirds of what Alex found when he discovered the full bowl, and 18 is two-thirds of 27.

358. 1 and 9. $1 \times 9 = 9$, $1 + 9 = 10$.

359. 1, 2, and 3. $1 + 2 + 3 = 6$ and $1 \times 2 \times 3 = 6$.

360. 18. Mr. Malik's back bumper, the front bumper of the 10th car, and the front and back bumpers of the eight cars between them.

361. 100. $\frac{9}{10}$ of $1000 = 900$, $\frac{8}{9}$ of $900 = 800$, $\frac{7}{8}$ of $800 = 700$, ..., $\frac{1}{2}$ of $200 = 100$.

362. Start by cooking the first side of burgers 1 and 2. After five minutes, flip over burger 1, set burger 2 aside, and begin cooking burger 3. After five more minutes, remove burger 1 (it's now fully cooked), flip burger 3, and return burger 2 to the grill to finish the uncooked side. In five more minutes, all three burgers will be fully cooked, and the total cook time is 15 minutes.

363. Just after 12. She must have arrived to hear the last chime from the 12 o'clock chimes. The next chime she heard was the half-hour chime at 12:30, and the final chime was the chime indicating one o'clock.

364. Harper is 14 and her mother is 41.

365. Three: he has one dog, one cat, and one bird.

366. Three. If you only pick up two socks, one might be white and the other gray. When you pick up a third sock, it will either be white or gray and match one of the first two socks you drew no matter what.

367. 10 cents. Most people will guess 20 cents, assuming the pencil costs $1, but since it costs $1 MORE than the eraser, that math doesn't work (i.e., if the eraser is 20 cents, the pencil would be $1.20 and together they would cost $1.40). Thus, the eraser is only 10 cents, the pencil is $1.10, and together they are $1.20.

368. E = 0, N = 3, O = 4, H = 5, T = 6, U = 7, F = 9

369. Two minutes. Each child will sharpen four pencils (12 pencils divided by three children). Each pencil takes 30 seconds to sharpen. Since each child has their own sharpener and thus can sharpen simultaneously, it will take them 30 seconds for each of their four pencils for a total of two minutes.

370. Kai collected five shark teeth and Carmen collected seven.

371. 200 feet. For every three feet Kabir moves forward, he is traveling 4 feet to make up for the backslide. Since the hill is 150 feet tall, he'll be making up 50 feet (150 feet divided by 3 feet equals 50, the number of times Kabir will backslide). Thus, Kabir will travel 150 feet plus an additional 50 feet to make up for the backslides every 3 feet.

372. Once the water starts boiling, she can start both the 3-minute timer and 10-minute timer. As soon as the 3-minute timer runs out, she can add the tea to the boiling water. The 10-minute timer will have seven minutes left at that point, so as soon as it runs out, her tea will be done.

373. 28. Each number in the sequence is the previous number plus the position of the current number. The last number is in the seventh position, so it is 21 + 7.

374. The first bag contains 22 pennies, the next bag contains 24, the third bag contains 26, and the fourth bag contains 28 pennies. 22 + 24 + 26 + 28 = 100 (The equation would look like this: $x + (x + 2) + (x + 4) + (x + 6) = 100$; solve for x).

375. More likely. You know you aren't holding the bag with two black marbles, so you're holding either the bag with two white marbles or the one with one white marble and one black marble. Out of three remaining marbles in those two bags, two are white. Therefore, you have a two-thirds chance of drawing a white marble, and a one-third chance that it will be black.

376. Yes, the rabbit will *just* make it to the hole in time. The rabbit will take 10 seconds to reach the hole (40 yards at 4 yards per second). Though the fox is moving faster, it will have to first make up the 10 yards between it and the rabbit. It will reach the rabbit's hole at the exact moment the rabbit does, 10 seconds into the chase (50 yards at 5 yards per second).

377. A = 2, B = 1, C = 3. This problem is easier than it appears. Since there are only three digits, we can determine 1, 2, and 3 simply by looking at the first letter in each of the numbers (representing the thousands position). B < A < C, which means C must be the largest digit (3) and B must be the smallest (1).

378. It takes five days. On day one she places 162 cards, on day two she adds 108 more cards (total cards placed = 270), on day three she adds 72 more cards (total = 342), on day four she added 48 more (total = 390), and on day five she adds the remaining 26 cards (total =416). For pure math, two-thirds of 48 would have been 32, but at that point she only had 26 cards remaining.

379. 4,632.

380. $4 \times 3 \div 6 + 8 - 1 = 9$

381. $2.50. Together they spent $7 so each should pay $3.50. Omar has already paid $1 so just owes the difference ($3.50 − $1 = $2.50).

382. 18. For each set of numbers, the second number is subtracted from the first number and then doubled to calculate the third number $(4 - 3 = 1, 1 \times 2 = 2; 10 - 6 = 4,$ $4 \times 2 = 8; 15 - 7 = 8, 8 \times 2 = 16; 7 - 5 = 2, 2 \times 2 = 4; 8 - 1 = 7, 7 \times 2 = 14;$ $12 - 3 = 9, 9 \times 2 = 18).$

BRAIN BENDER

383. Emery will always out-earn Theo. During the first three months, Theo will make $5 + $6 + $7 = $18. Emery will make $2.50 + $2.75 + $3.00 + $3.25 + $3.50 + $3.75 = $18.75. Continuing for the rest of the year, Theo will make $18 (from the first three months) + $8 + $9 + $10 + $11 + $12 + $13 + $14 + $15 + $16 = $126. Emery will earn $18.75 + $4.00 + $4.25 + $4.50 + $4.75 + $5.00 + $5.25 + $5.50 + $5.75 + $6.00 + $6.25 + $6.50 + $6.75 + $7.00 + $7.25 + $7.50 + $7.75 + $8.00 + $8.25 = $129.

Chapter 6: Logic Puzzles

384. TALK → TASK

385. Samir prefers math, Kendall prefers reading, Harley prefers music, Eden prefers science, and Drew prefers social studies. We know Harley and Drew's favorites from clues 2 and 4, which leaves math, reading, and science for the remaining friends. Eden likes math or science, but since neither Samir nor Kendall likes science, Eden's favorite must be science. Since Samir dislikes reading, math is the only possibility left as her favorite, leaving Kendall with reading.

386. The letter *E*: cheat, below, reset.

387. Finger. A scarf is something you wear around your neck. A ring is something you wear on your finger.

388. Paris plays soccer, Raven plays baseball, and Corey plays basketball.

389. Tuesday.

390. Mila, Lulu, Dani, Owen, Elijah.

391. The person from Kenya (who lives in the blue house) owns the fish.

392. First, he must take the rabbit across and return alone. Next, he brings the lettuce across. He leaves the lettuce on that side of the river but returns with the rabbit. Once back, he swaps the rabbit for the dog and brings the dog across. Then, he returns alone to fetch the rabbit.

393. Three students were wearing solid colored shirts. No students were wearing solid red shirts ($12 - 8 - 3 - 1 = 0$). One student was wearing a solid blue shirt ($10 - 8 - 1 = 1$). Two students were wearing solid yellow shirts ($6 - 3 - 1 = 2$). Zero solid red shirts plus 1 solid blue shirt plus 2 solid yellow shirts equals 3 solid colored shirts.

394. No. Since all peanut-filled candies are red, and Jules does not like red candies but does like all the candies in the bowl, there must not be any red candies in the bowl; thus, there are no candies with peanuts inside in the bowl.

395. The category is NUMBER and the words are EIGHT, NINE, and TEN.

396. Joyce's favorite color is blue and she likes oranges best. Ruby's favorite color is green (the only one that is a blend of two colors), and she prefers bananas. Isaac's favorite color is yellow and his favorite fruit is kiwi. (We know because yellow and blue are the only colors that mix to make Ruby's green. His fruit can't be yellow, so it has to be kiwi.) Camilla's favorite color is red, and she loves cherries. (They match colors.)

397. PLANE → PLANT

398. Orchard. An acorn grows into a tree, which is part of a forest, just as a seed grows into a fruit tree, which is part of an orchard.

399. The letter *G*: rugby, thing, surge.

400. Yard and beak.

401. Chloe and Amit cross first in two minutes. Then Chloe returns alone in one minute. Next, Maliah and Oliver cross together in eight minutes. Amit returns with the flashlight to retrieve Chloe, taking two minutes each way. $2 + 1 + 8 + 2 + 2 = 15$.

402. Moisture. If someone is hungry, they lack food. If something is dry, it lacks moisture.

403. Remove an item from the "PENCILS & ERASERS" bin. If it's a pencil, that bin should be labeled "PENCILS" since we know that the "PENCILS & ERASERS" is incorrect and yet the bin contains pencils. The bin labeled "PENCILS" should be labeled "ERASERS" because if it contains pencils and erasers then the third bin would be labeled "ERASERS" and contain erasers, which isn't possible since we know *all* three bins are mislabeled. Thus, the first bin should be "PENCILS," the second bin "ERASERS," and the third bin "PENCILS & ERASERS." Similarly, if the first item you draw from the "PENCILS & ERASERS" bin is an eraser instead of a pencil, then it should be labeled "ERASERS," the bin labeled "ERASERS" should be labeled "PENCILS," and the bin labeled "PENCILS" should be labeled "PENCILS & ERASERS."

404. The two children must go across first. One child gets out, and the other returns. Upon returning, the child gets out and one of the parents crosses to the other side. Once there, the parent gets out and the child comes back in the boat to pick up the other child, and they return to the far side. One child gets out to wait with the parent while the other child crosses back to the start. The other parent now goes across, and the child there brings the boat back to pick up the other child; they both cross to the far side together. Although the family is together, they must still return the boat to the fisherman on the other side so one child comes back, gets out, and lets the fisherman cross. Once across, the fisherman gets out, the child gets in and returns to pick up the other child. They return to the far side where the fisherman gets in his boat to go on his way, while the family continues their backpacking adventure.

405. Deep and shallow.

406. COOL → POOL

407. WARM → WARD → CARD → CORD → COLD

408. Stir and teen.

409. Sweep. A pencil is used to write. A broom is used to sweep.

410. Dominique is turning 5 and getting a video game, Aidan is turning 10 and getting a bike. Yuki is turning 8 and getting a puppy. Zara is turning 12 and getting clothes.

411. The category is DRINK and the words are MILK, WATER, and JUICE.

412. Soda and lily.

413. Violet was wearing a magenta dress, Magenta was wearing a rose dress, and Rose was wearing a violet dress. We know Violet was wearing magenta because she couldn't be wearing violet (none of the girls' dresses matched their names), and we know she wasn't wearing rose because the girl wearing the rose-colored dress answered her.

414. The letter *H:* thank, aches, lather.

415. Parent. A sister is, by definition, a sibling. A father is, by definition, a parent.

416. First, one boy and one girl must cross, and the girl must return with the boat. Then, two boys can cross, with one boy making the return trip. Next, two girls will cross, and a boy and a girl return. Now, two girls cross, and one boy returns. He goes back and forth twice to pick up each remaining boy.

417. Header and footer.

418. HEAD → READ → ROAD → TOAD → TOED → TOES

419. GHOST → HOST

420. Luciana = blue Bobcats, Langston = yellow Raptors, Levi = orange Eagles, Lincoln = purple Pythons, Lillian = red Firebirds. We know from the third clue that Levi's jersey is orange and that he plays for the Eagles. The fourth clue reveals that Langston and Lillian's jerseys must be red and yellow. The only other colors that can combine to create one of the listed jersey colors are red and blue to make purple. We already know Lillian's color must be red or yellow, so it can't be blue, and thus must be red, meaning that Luciana's jersey must be blue. From the first clue, we know Luciana's team name starts with the same letter as her jersey color, so Luciana's team must be the Bobcats. Since Lillian's jersey is red, Langston's jersey must be yellow. Following the color combination logic, we know Lincoln's jersey must be purple (red + blue) and from the first clue, we know his team must be the Pythons. That leaves just the Firebirds and the Raptors for Langston and Lillian. From the second clue, we know Langston is not on the Firebirds, and thus must be a Raptor, meaning Lillian must be a Firebird.

421. The category is SENSES and the words are TOUCH, SIGHT, and SMELL.

422. Tidal wave. Breeze is a light wind, while a tornado is a devastating wind. A trickle is a small flow of water, while a tidal wave is a devastating flow of water.

423. Smart, clever, and brainy.

424. Pass and fail.

425. Ariel owns the pizza truck on Dominican Dr. that sells 7 items. Bailey owns the gyros truck on River Rd. that sells 4 items. Cameron owns the hot dog truck on Charles Ct. that sells 5 items. Devon owns the salad truck on Apple Ave. that sells 8 items. And Riley owns the taco truck on Badger Blvd. that sells 6 items.

We know from the second clue that Ariel must sell pizza or gyros. Since we know from the third clue that Bailey sells gyros, Ariel must sell pizza. We also know from the second clue that Ariel sells 7 items and Devon sells 8. We know from the fifth clue that Devon must sell salads, meaning Cameron and Riley must sell hot dogs and tacos, though we don't know who sells which yet. From the eighth clue, we know that Riley sells more than Cameron, and from the third clue we know Bailey sells less than Cameron, so Bailey must sell only 4 items, Cameron must sell 5, and Riley must sell 6. From the seventh clue, we know that the truck on River Rd. must be Bailey's gyros. The first clue rules out the possibility of Riley selling hot dogs, meaning Cameron must sell them and is parked on Charles Ct. Riley must sell tacos, and we know from the fourth clue that the taco truck is on Badger Blvd. Again from the first clue, we know that Ariel can't be parked on Apple Ave., so that must be where Devon's truck is, leaving Dominican Dr. as the only possibility for Ariel's truck. We know from the seventh clue that the truck on River Rd. must sell gyros. It can't be Devon's salads since it sells fewer items than the hot dog truck. Thus, Bailey owns the truck on River Rd.

From the last clue, we know the pizza truck must belong to Cameron, and Riley must sell hot dogs. From the first clue, we know that Riley's truck is parked on River Rd.

About the Authors

CAROLE P. ROMAN is the award-winning author of more than 50 children's books. Whether about pirates, princesses, or discovering the world around us, her books have enchanted educators, parents, and her diverse audience of children. She hosts a blog radio program and is one of the founders of a new magazine, *Indie Author's Monthly.*

CORINNE SCHMITT is the author of *Super Fun Family Card Games* and the blogger behind *Wondermom Wannabe.* She is an avid fan of riddles, puzzles, and brain teasers. Corinne graduated from the University of Illinois with a degree in English literature and a master's in business administration. She is married to a retired US Marine and has five children, all of whom share her love of riddles. She currently resides in Northern Virginia.

About the Illustrator

DYLAN GOLDBERGER is an illustrator and printmaker based in Brooklyn, New York. He grew up in New Rochelle and moved to Brooklyn in 2007 to attend Pratt Institute, graduating with a BFA in communication design. His self-published alphabet book, *See Spot Shred*, released in 2015, reveals his love of dogs and skateboarding, recurring themes throughout his artwork. When he's not working in the studio, he's out exploring the parks and streets of New York City with his dog Townes. His illustrations have been used by many notable brands and publications.